⁛⁛studysync®

Reading & Writing Companion

Personal Best

What qualities of character matter most?

studysync.com

Send all inquiries to:
BookheadEd Learning, LLC
610 Daniel Young Drive
Sonoma, CA 95476

ISBN 978-1-94-469576-7

1 2 3 4 5 6 QVS 24 23 22 21 20 19

A

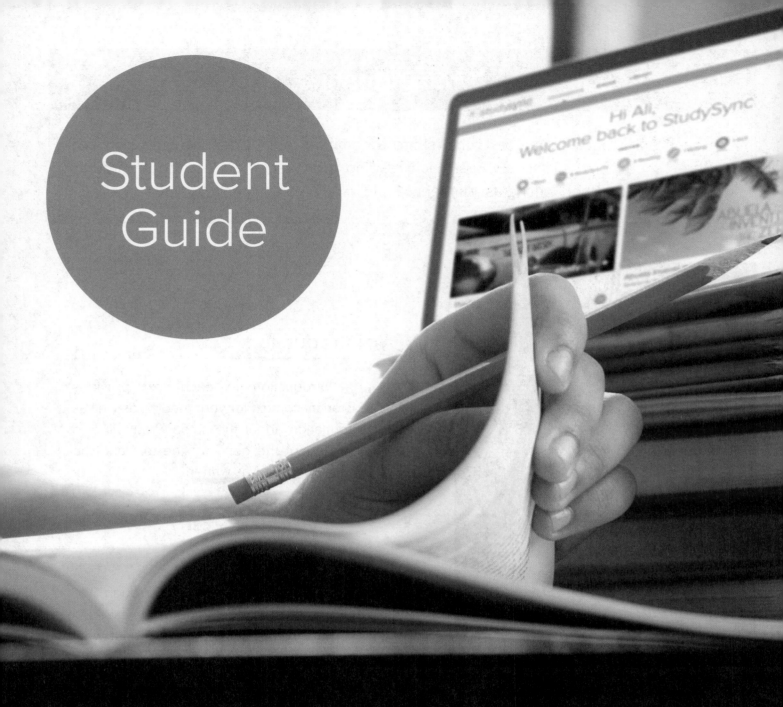

Student Guide

Getting Started

Welcome to the StudySync Reading & Writing Companion! In this book, you will find a collection of readings based on the theme of the unit you are studying. As you work through the readings, you will be asked to answer questions and perform a variety of tasks designed to help you closely analyze and understand each text selection. Read on for an explanation of each

Close Reading and Writing Routine

In each unit, you will read texts that share a common theme, despite their different genres, time periods, and authors. Each reading encourages a closer look through questions and a short writing assignment.

Eleven

FICTION
Sandra Cisneros
1991

Introduction   **study**sync●

andra Cisneros (b. 1954) is a renowned Chicana writer whose poems, novels, and short stories explore the complicated struggle of finding one's own identity. Cisneros is best known for her novel *The House on Mango Street* and the collection *Woman Hollering Creek and Other Stories*. "Eleven" is from the latter, the story of a girl named Rachel who experiences growing pains on her eleventh birthday. When her teacher insists that an ugly red sweater belongs to Rachel, the eleven-year-old has exceptional thoughts but can't share them. Even so, it's evident that the protagonist of Sandra Cisneros's short story has insight beyond her years.

Eleven

"You open your eyes and everything's
just like yesterday, only it's today.
And you don't feel eleven at all."

What they don't understand about birthdays and what they never tell you is that when you're eleven, you're also ten, and nine, and eight, and seven, and six, and five, and four, and three, and two, and one. And when you wake up on your eleventh birthday you expect to feel eleven, but you don't. You open your eyes and everything's just like yesterday, only it's today. And you don't feel eleven at all. You feel like you're still ten. And you are—underneath the year that makes you eleven.

Like some days you might say something stupid, and that's the part of you that's still ten. Or maybe some days you might need to sit on your mama's lap because you're scared, and that's the part of you that's five. And maybe one day when you're all grown up maybe you will need to cry like if you're three, and that's okay. That's what I tell Mama when she's sad and needs to cry. Maybe she's feeling three.

Because the way you grow old is kind of like an onion or like the rings inside a tree trunk or like my little wooden dolls that fit one inside the other, each year inside the next one. That's how being eleven years old is.

You don't feel eleven. Not right away. It takes a few days, weeks even, sometimes even months before you say Eleven when they ask you. And you don't feel smart eleven, not until you're almost twelve. That's the way it is.

Only today I wish I didn't have only eleven years rattling inside me like pennies in a tin Band-Aid box. Today I wish I was one hundred and two instead of eleven because if I was one hundred and two I'd have known what to say when Mrs. Price put the red sweater on my desk. I would've known how to tell her it wasn't mine instead of just sitting there with that look on my face and nothing coming out of my mouth.

"Whose is this?" Mrs. Price says, and she holds the red sweater up in the air for all the class to see. "Whose? It's been sitting in the coatroom for a month."

 Skill: Figurative
Language

The narrator uses similes when she compares aging to everyday things. When I picture onions, tree trunks, and wooden dolls, I notice they all have layers. She must mean that when you get older, you keep getting more layers.

① Introduction

An Introduction to each text provides historical context for your reading as well as information about the author. You will also learn about the genre of the text and the year in which it was written.

② Notes

Many times, while working through the activities after each text, you will be asked to **annotate** or **make annotations** about what you are reading. This means that you should highlight or underline words in the text and use the "Notes" column to make comments or jot down any questions you have. You may also want to note any unfamiliar vocabulary words here.

You will also see sample student annotations to go along with the Skill lesson for that text.

First Read

During your first reading of each selection, you should just try to get a general idea of the content and message of the reading. Don't worry if there are parts you don't understand or words that are unfamiliar to you. You'll have an opportunity later to dive deeper into the text.

Think Questions

These questions will ask you to start thinking critically about the text, asking specific questions about its purpose, and making connections to your prior knowledge and reading experiences. To answer these questions, you should go back to the text and draw upon specific evidence to support your responses. You will also begin to explore some of the more challenging vocabulary words in the selection.

Skills

Each Skill includes two parts: Checklist and Your Turn. In the Checklist, you will learn the process for analyzing the text. The model student annotations in the text provide examples of how you might make your own notes following the instructions in the Checklist. In the Your Turn, you will use those same instructions to practice the skill.

First Read

Read "Eleven." After you read, complete the Think Questions below.

THINK QUESTIONS

1. How does Rachel feel about the red sweater that is placed on her desk? Respond with textual evidence from the story as well as ideas that you have inferred from clues in the text.

2. According to Rachel, why does Sylvia say the sweater belongs to Rachel? Support your answer with textual evidence.

3. Write two or three sentences exploring why Mrs. Price responds as she does when Phyllis claims the sweater. Support your answer with textual evidence.

4. Find the word **raggedy** in paragraph 9 of "Eleven." Use context clues in the surrounding sentences, as well as the sentence in which the word appears, to determine the word's meaning. Write your definition here and identify clues that helped you figure out its meaning.

5. Use context clues to determine the meaning of **nonsense** as it is used in paragraph 15 of "Eleven." Write your definition here and identify clues that helped you figure out its meaning. Then check the meaning in a dictionary.

Skill:
Figurative Language

Use the Checklist to analyze Figurative Language in "Eleven." Refer to the sample student annotations about Figurative Language in the text.

CHECKLIST FOR FIGURATIVE LANGUAGE

To determine the meaning of figures of speech in a text, note the following:

✓ words that mean one thing literally and suggest something else

✓ similes, such as "strong as an ox"

✓ metaphors, such as "her eyes were stars"

✓ personification, such as "the daisies danced in the wind"

In order to interpret the meaning of a figure of speech in context, ask the following questions:

✓ Does any of the descriptive language in the text compare two seemingly unlike things?

✓ Do any descriptions include "like" or "as" that indicate a simile?

✓ Is there a direct comparison that suggests a metaphor?

✓ Is a human quality is being used to describe this animal, object, force of nature or idea that suggests personification?

✓ How does the use of this figure of speech change your understanding of the thing or person being described?

YOUR TURN

1. How does the figurative language in paragraph 18 help readers understand Rachel's reaction to the sweater?

   ○ A. The metaphors in the paragraph help readers understand how uncomfortable Rachel feels in the sweater.
   ○ B. The similes in the paragraph help readers understand how uncomfortable Rachel feels in the sweater.
   ○ C. The metaphors in the paragraph make it clear to readers that Rachel is overreacting about the sweater.
   ○ D. The similes in the paragraph make it clear to readers that Rachel is overreacting about the sweater.

2. How does the figurative language in paragraph 19 help readers visualize Rachel's behavior?

   ○ A. The mention of "little animal noises" tells readers that Rachel is acting more like an animal than a human.
   ○ B. The metaphor of "clown-sweater arms" shows that Rachel is able to see the humorous side in her experience.
   ○ C. The similes about her body shaking "like when you have the hiccups" and her head hurting "like when you drink milk too fast" connect to unpleasant experiences most readers have had.
   ○ D. The statement that "there aren't any more tears left in [her] eyes" suggests that Rachel is starting to calm down.

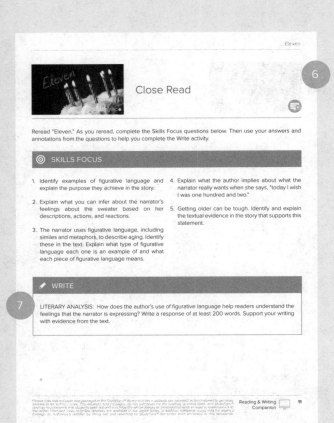

Close Read

Reread "Eleven." As you reread, complete the Skills Focus questions below. Then use your answers and annotations from the questions to help you complete the Write activity.

◎ SKILLS FOCUS

1. Identify examples of figurative language and explain the purpose they achieve in the story.

2. Explain what you can infer about the narrator's feelings about the sweater based on her descriptions, actions, and reactions.

3. The narrator uses figurative language, including similes and metaphors, to describe aging. Identify these in the text. Explain what type of figurative language each one is an example of and what each piece of figurative language means.

4. Explain what the author implies about what the narrator really wants when she says, "today I wish I was one hundred and two."

5. Getting older can be tough. Identify and explain the textual evidence in the story that supports this statement.

✎ WRITE

LITERARY ANALYSIS: How does the author's use of figurative language help readers understand the feelings that the narrator is expressing? Write a response of at least 200 words. Support your writing with evidence from the text.

Lost Island

FICTION

Introduction

Marina wakes up alone, thirsty, and hungry on a deserted island. How did she get here, and why is her head throbbing? As she slowly recalls a large wave smashing into Uncle Merlin's fishing boat, Marina takes her first steps towards survival.

▼ VOCABULARY

damp
wet

capsized
tipped over in the water

intense
very strong

rescuer
someone who saves a person from harm or danger

---

⑥ Close Read & Skills Focus

After you have completed the First Read, you will be asked to go back and read the text more closely and critically. Before you begin your Close Read, you should read through the Skills Focus to get an idea of the concepts you will want to focus on during your second reading. You should work through the Skills Focus by making annotations, highlighting important concepts, and writing notes or questions in the "Notes" column. Depending on instructions from your teacher, you may need to respond online or use a separate piece of paper to start expanding on your thoughts and ideas.

⑦ Write

Your study of each selection will end with a writing assignment. For this assignment, you should use your notes, annotations, personal ideas, and answers to both the Think and Skills Focus. Be sure to read the prompt carefully and address each part of it in your writing.

⑧ English Language Learner

The English Language Learner texts focus on improving language proficiency. You will practice learning strategies and skills in individual and group activities to become better readers, writers, and speakers.

Extended Writing Project

This is your opportunity to use genre characteristics and craft to compose meaningful, longer written works exploring the theme of each unit. You will draw information from your readings, research, and own life experiences to complete the assignment.

1 Writing Project

After you have read all of the unit text selections, you will move on to a writing project. Each project will guide you through the process of writing your essay. Student models will provide guidance and help you organize your thoughts. One unit ends with an **Extended Oral Project** which will give you an opportunity to develop your oral language and communication skills.

2 Writing Process Steps

There are four steps in the writing process: Plan, Draft, Revise, and Edit and Publish. During each step, you will form and shape your writing project, and each lesson's peer review will give you the chance to receive feedback from your peers and teacher.

3 Writing Skills

Each Skill lesson focuses on a specific strategy or technique that you will use during your writing project. Each lesson presents a process for applying the skill to your own work and gives you the opportunity to practice it to improve your writing.

Personal Best

What qualities of character matter most?

> Genre Focus: ARGUMENTATIVE TEXT

Texts

 Comparing Within and Across Genres

Extended Writing Project: Argumentative Writing

English Language Learner Resources

What qualities of character matter most?

RAY BRADBURY

American author Ray Bradbury (1920–2012) was fourteen when his family moved from Illinois to an apartment in the middle of Hollywood. Bradbury roller-skated to movie premieres and dreamed of becoming a writer. A few years later, he published his first story and began his distinguished career as an author of fantasy, horror, mystery, and science fiction. Bradbury's influence extended beyond literature, and he was consulted by Disney in the design of Epcot and flown to Cape Canaveral by NASA to lecture astronauts.

RUSSELL FREEDMAN

As a reporter and editor for the Associated Press in San Francisco, Russell Freedman (1929–2018) gained experience in research and writing that prepared him for his second career as an author of nonfiction, which he began in the 1950s when he moved to New York City. His biographies illuminated the lives of historical figures—Abraham Lincoln, Marco Polo, Tasunke Witco (more commonly known as Crazy Horse), and Eleanor Roosevelt, to name a few—who were motivated to challenge injustice.

NAOMI SHIHAB NYE

"Where we live in the world is never one place," writes Naomi Shihab Nye (b. 1952), who grew up between Ferguson, Missouri, near where her American mother was raised, and Jerusalem, her father's Palestinian homeland. The poet, essayist, and songwriter currently lives in San Antonio, Texas. Nye began writing poems at the age of six, and says she loves to write anywhere—at home, outdoors, or even at the airport.

RICHARD PECK

Novelist Richard Peck (1934–2018) gathered material for some of his stories from his brief career as an English teacher at a junior high in Illinois. "Ironically, it was my students who taught me to be a writer, though I was hired to teach them," Peck said after winning the Newbery Medal in 2001 for his book *A Year Down Yonder.* For nearly fifty years Peck lived in New York City, writing for children and young adults, and composing all of his works on the typewriter.

KURT VONNEGUT

Kurt Vonnegut (1922–2007) was an American author of novels, short stories, plays, and essays from Indianapolis, Indiana. In 1943, he dropped out of Cornell University and enlisted in the US Army to fight in World War II. He was captured during the Battle of the Bulge and taken to a prison camp in Dresden, where took refuge in the meatlocker of a slaughterhouse during the bombing of the city by Allied forces. This experience forms the plot of the first chapter of his most famous novel, *Slaughterhouse-Five* (1969).

MALALA YOUSAFZAI

When Malala Yousafzai (b. 1997) was just eleven years old, she said goodbye to her classmates in Mingora, Pakistan, unsure when or if she would ever see them again. It was 2008, and the Taliban had just seized control of Yousafzai's village in Swat Valley, and, among many new rules, girls were no longer allowed to go to school. Yousafzai, an activist, writer, and Nobel laureate, has since dedicated her life to creating "a world where girls are empowered to reach their potential through a quality education."

LYNNE OLSON

Former US Secretary of State Madeleine Albright called American author and historian Lynne Olson (b. 1949) "our era's foremost chronicler of World War II politics and diplomacy." Olson, who was born in Hawaii, was a journalist for a decade before becoming a full-time author. She wrote national features for the Associated Press and reported on national politics and the White House for the Baltimore Sun. She currently lives in Washington, DC.

I Am Malala:
The Girl Who Stood Up
for Education and
Was Shot by the Taliban

INFORMATIONAL TEXT
Malala Yousafzai
2013

Introduction

A champion of education from an early age, Malala Yousafzai (b. 1997) survived a gunshot wound to the head at age 15 inflicted by a Taliban gunman. At age 17, Malala became the youngest person to receive the Nobel Peace Prize. In this excerpt from her memoir, Malala, age eleven, lives with her parents and two younger brothers in the Swat Valley of Northern Pakistan, which has come under control of Taliban extremists. Incensed by the Taliban's mandate that all girls' schools in the Swat Valley must close by January 15, 2009, Malala takes a risky, conspicuous public stance against the Taliban, using radio, TV, a blog, and a diary written under the pseudonym Gul Makai (for which this chapter is titled) to relay her message.

"Education is neither Eastern nor Western. It is human."

from Chapter 13: The Diary of Gul Makai

1   We had a special assembly that final morning, but it was hard to hear with the noise of helicopters overhead. Some of us spoke out against what was happening in our valley. The bell rang for the very last time, and then Madam Maryam announced it was winter vacation. But unlike in other years no date was announced for the start of next term. Even so, some teachers still gave us homework. In the yard I hugged all my friends. I looked at the honors board and wondered if my name would ever appear on it again. Exams were due in March, but how could they take place? Coming first didn't matter if you couldn't study at all. When someone takes away your pens you realize quite how important education is.

2   Before I closed the school door I looked back as if it were the last time I would ever be at school. That's the closing door in one part of the documentary. In reality I went back inside. My friends and I didn't want that day to end, so we decided to stay on for a while longer. We went to the primary school where there was more space to run around and played cops and robbers. Then we played mango mango, where you make a circle and sing, then when the song stops everyone has to freeze. Anyone who moves or laughs is out.

3   We came home from school late that day. Usually we leave at 1 p.m., but that day we stayed till three. Before we left, Moniba and I had an argument over something so silly I can't remember what it was. Our friends couldn't believe it. "You two always argue when there's an important occasion!" they said. It wasn't a good way to leave things.

4   I told the documentary makers, "They cannot stop me. I will get my education if it's at home, school, or somewhere else. This is our request to the world—to save our schools, save our Pakistan, save our Swat."

5   When I got home, I cried and cried. I didn't want to stop learning. I was only eleven years old, but I felt as though I had lost everything. I had told everyone in my class that the Taliban wouldn't go through with it. "They're just like our politicians—they talk the talk, but they won't do anything," I'd said. But then

**Skill:
Connotation
and Denotation**

*I can look at context
clues to determine the
denotation of the word
income. I notice that
Malala says that the
school closing is a loss
of business for her dad,
and she mentions fees,
money and bills that her
dad had to take care
of. I think income means
how much money her
family makes.*

**Skill: Author's
Purpose and
Point of View**

*Malala's purpose is to
criticize the Taliban and
persuade readers to
agree with her views
about education. She
thinks education should
be available to all. She
makes it clear by using
short, clear sentences
full of emotion to share
her opinion.*

they went ahead and closed our school and I felt embarrassed. I couldn't control myself. I was crying, my mother was crying, but my father insisted, "You will go to school."

6 For him the closing of the schools also meant the loss of business. The boys' school would reopen after the holidays, but the loss of the girls' school **represented** a big cut in our income. More than half the school fees were overdue, and my father spent the last day chasing money to pay the rent, the utility bills and the teachers' salaries.

7 That night the air was full of artillery fire and I woke up three times. The next morning everything had changed. I began to think that maybe I should go to Peshawar[1] or abroad or maybe I could ask our teachers to form a secret school in our home, as some Afghans had done during Taliban rule. Afterward I went on as many radio and TV channels as possible. "They can stop us going to school, but they can't stop us learning," I said. I sounded hopeful, but in my heart I was worried. My father and I went to Peshawar and visited lots of places to tell people what was happening. I spoke of the irony of the Taliban wanting female teachers and doctors for women yet not letting girls go to school to qualify for these jobs.

8 Once Muslim Khan had said girls should not go to school and learn Western ways. This from a man who had lived so long in America! He insisted he would have his own education system. "What would Muslim Khan use instead of the stethoscope and the thermometer?" my father asked. "Are there any Eastern instruments that will treat the sick?" The Taliban is against education because they think that when a child reads a book or learns English or studies science he or she will become **Westernized**.

9 But I said, "Education is education. We should learn everything and then choose which path to follow." Education is neither Eastern nor Western. It is human."

10 My mother used to tell me to hide my face when I spoke to the media because at my age I should be in purdah[2] and she was afraid for my safety. But she never banned me from doing anything. It was a time of horror and fear. People often said the Taliban would kill my father but not me. "Malala is a child," they would say, "and even the Taliban don't kill children."

11 But my grandmother wasn't so sure. Whenever my grandmother saw me speaking on television, or leaving the house, she would pray, "Please God make Malala like Benazir Bhutto but do not give her Benazir's short life."

---

1. **Peshawar** Pakistani city near the Khyber Pass
2. **purdah** the practice of covering and segregation of women in Muslim and Hindu cultures

12 After my school closed down, I continued to write the blog. Four days after the ban on girls' schools, five more were destroyed. "I'm quite surprised," I wrote, "because these schools had closed, so why did they also need to be destroyed? No one has gone to school following the Taliban's deadline. The army is doing nothing about it. They are sitting in their bunkers on top of the hills. They slaughter goats and eat with pleasure." I also wrote about people going to watch the **floggings** announced on Mullah FM, and the fact that the army and police were nowhere to be seen.

13 One day we got a call from America, from a student at Stanford University. Her name was Shiza Shahid and she came from Islamabad. She had seen the *New York Times* documentary *Class Dismissed in Swat Valley* and tracked us down. We saw then the power of the media and she became a great support to us. My father was almost bursting with pride at how I came across in the documentary. "Look at her," he told Adam Ellick. "Don't you think she is meant for the skies?" Fathers can be very embarrassing.

14 Adam took us to Islamabad. It was the first time I had ever visited. Islamabad was a beautiful place with nice white bungalows and broad roads, though it has none of the natural beauty of Swat. We saw the Red Mosque where the **siege** had taken place, the buildings of the Parliament House and the Presidency, where Zardari now lived. General Musharraf was in exile in London.

15 We went to shops where I bought school books and Adam bought me DVDs of American TV programs like *Ugly Betty,* which was about a girl with big braces and a big heart. I loved it and dreamed of one day going to New York and working on a magazine like her. We visited the Lok Virsa museum, and it was a joy to celebrate our national **heritage** once again. Our own museum in Swat had closed. On the steps outside an old man was selling popcorn. He was a Pashtun[3] like us, and when my father asked if he was from Islamabad he replied, "Do you think Islamabad can ever belong to us Pashtuns?" He said he came from Mohmand, one of the tribal areas, but had to flee because of a military operation. I saw tears in my parents' eyes.

16 Lots of buildings were surrounded by concrete blocks, and there were checkpoints for incoming vehicles to guard against suicide bombs. When our bus hit a pothole on our way back my brother Khushal, who had been asleep, jerked awake. "Was that a bomb blast?" he asked. This was the fear that filled our daily lives. Any small disturbance or noise could be a bomb or gunfire.

Excerpted from *I Am Malala: The Girl Who Stood Up for Education and Was Shot by the Taliban* by Malala Yousafzai, published by Back Bay Books

---

3. **Pashtun** members of the Pashto people living in Afghanistan and Pakistan

NOTES

Skill: Author's Purpose and Point of View

Malala's attitude toward the police is clear. Her point of view is that the police and army were failing in their duty to protect the people by allowing the Taliban to terrorize her city.

Please note that excerpts and passages in the StudySync® library and this workbook are intended as touchstones to generate interest in an author's work. The excerpts and passages do not substitute for the reading of entire texts, and StudySync® strongly recommends that students seek out and purchase the whole literary or informational work in order to experience it as the author intended. Links to online resellers are available in our digital library. In addition, complete works may be ordered through an authorized reseller by filling out and returning to StudySync® the order form enclosed in this workbook.

Reading & Writing Companion   3

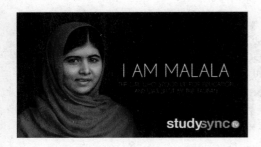

First Read

Read "I Am Malala: The Girl Who Stood Up for Education and Was Shot by the Taliban." After you read, complete the Think Questions below.

☁ THINK QUESTIONS

1. How does Malala respond to the closing of her school? Use specific examples from the text in your answer.

2. Based on the text, why does the Taliban condemn the education of girls and not the education of boys? What can you infer about the Taliban's values?

3. How do Malala's relatives feel about her choice to speak up for the right of girls to education? Use specific examples from the text in your answer.

4. Read the following dictionary entry:

   siege

   siege /sēj/ *noun*

   1. An attack in which an army surrounds a group of people or city to get them to surrender
   2. An illness
   3. Any general attempt to gain control

   Which definition most closely matches the meaning of **siege** as it is used in paragraph 14? Write the correct definition of *siege* here and explain how you figured out the correct meaning.

5. Use context clues to determine the meaning of the word **heritage** as it is used in paragraph 15. Write your definition of *heritage* here and explain how context clues in the paragraph led to your understanding of the word's meaning.

Skill: Author's Purpose and Point of View

Use the Checklist to analyze Author's Purpose and Point of View in "I Am Malala: The Girl Who Stood Up for Education and Was Shot by the Taliban." Refer to the sample student annotations about Author's Purpose and Point of View in the text.

••• CHECKLIST FOR AUTHOR'S PURPOSE AND POINT OF VIEW

In order to identify an author's purpose and point of view, note the following:

✓ facts, statistics, and graphic aids as these indicate that the author is writing to inform

✓ the author's use of emotional or figurative language, which may indicate that the author is trying to persuade readers or stress an opinion

✓ descriptions that present a complicated process in plain language, which may indicate that the author is writing to explain

✓ the language the author uses, as figurative and emotional language can be clues to the author's point of view on a subject or topic

To determine the author's purpose and point of view in a text, consider the following questions:

✓ How does the author convey, or communicate, information in the text?

✓ Does the author use figurative or emotional language? For what purpose?

✓ Does the author make use of charts, graphs, maps and other graphic aids?

Please note that excerpts and passages in the StudySync® library and this workbook are intended as touchstones to generate interest in an author's work. The excerpts and passages do not substitute for the reading of entire texts, and StudySync® strongly recommends that students seek out and purchase the whole literary or informational work in order to experience it as the author intended. Links to online resellers are available in our digital library. In addition, complete works may be ordered through an authorized reseller by filling out and returning to StudySync® the order form enclosed in this workbook.

Reading & Writing Companion   **5**

Skill: Author's Purpose and Point of View

Reread paragraphs 14–15 from "I Am Malala: The Girl Who Stood Up for Education and Was Shot by the Taliban." Then, using the Checklist on the previous page, answer the multiple-choice questions below.

⟳ YOUR TURN

1. What is the author's purpose in telling readers about Islamabad in paragraph 14?

    ○ A. to persuade readers to visit the city

    ○ B. to describe the city so readers can visualize it

    ○ C. to inform readers about the origin of the city

    ○ D. to explain why Adam took the family to the city

2. Which of the following best describes the author's point of view in paragraph 15?

    ○ A. Malala feels safer in Islamabad.

    ○ B. Malala is angry that Islamabad is different from Swat.

    ○ C. Malala wishes her parents had not come with her to Islamabad.

    ○ D. Malala loves Islamabad and wishes her city could be more like it.

Skill:
Connotation and Denotation

Use the Checklist to analyze Connotation and Denotation in "I Am Malala: The Girl Who Stood Up for Education and Was Shot by the Taliban." Refer to the sample student annotations about Connotation and Denotation in the text.

••• CHECKLIST FOR CONNOTATION AND DENOTATION

In order to identify the denotative meanings of words and phrases, use the following steps:

✓ first, note unfamiliar words and phrases: key words used to describe important individuals, events or ideas, and words that inspire an emotional reaction

✓ next, verify the denotative meaning of unfamiliar words by consulting reference material such as a dictionary, glossary, or thesaurus

To better understand the meaning of words and phrases as they are used in a text, including connotative meanings, use the following questions:

✓ What is the genre or subject of the text? How does that affect the possible meaning of a word or phrase?

✓ Does the word create a positive, negative, or neutral emotion?

✓ What synonyms or alternative phrasings help you describe the connotative meaning of the word?

To determine the meaning of words and phrases as they are used in a text, including connotative meanings, use the following questions:

✓ What is the meaning of the word or phrase? What is the connotation as well as the denotation?

✓ If I substitute a synonym based on denotation, is the meaning the same? How does it change the meaning of the text?

Skill:
Connotation and Denotation

Reread paragraphs 10–11 from "I Am Malala: The Girl Who Stood Up for Education and Was Shot by the Taliban." Then, using the Checklist on the previous page, answer the multiple-choice questions below.

⟳ YOUR TURN

1. Based on the context clues in paragraph 10, what is most likely the denotative meaning of "purdah"?

   ○ A. being in a mosque
   ○ B. being out in the open
   ○ C. being with her mother
   ○ D. being in seclusion

2. What is the connotative meaning of the phrase "and even the Taliban don't kill children" in paragraph 10?

   ○ A. The Taliban have killed children.
   ○ B. Others kill children, but not the Taliban.
   ○ C. The Taliban is evil.
   ○ D. The Taliban plans to kill children.

Close Read

Reread "I Am Malala: The Girl Who Stood Up for Education and Was Shot by the Taliban." As you reread, complete the Skills Focus questions below. Then use your answers and annotations from the questions to help you complete the Write activity.

◎ SKILLS FOCUS

1. Identify places in the text where Malala's purpose is to persuade readers to accept her point of view on conditions in Swat. Explain what Malala wants readers to understand.

2. Identify specific words and phrases in the text that indicate Malala's negative feelings about the Taliban.

3. Identify passages in the text where Malala's purpose is to persuade readers that the media both supports her cause and endangers her at the same time.

4. Not everyone would stand up to the Taliban. Identify examples of the character qualities you think were most important in driving Malala to act. Explain your reasoning.

✎ WRITE

ARGUMENTATIVE: What message is Malala trying to convey about the media? According to the author, did it help or injure her, or both? In your response, cite specific examples of Malala's word choice that help the reader understand how she views the media.

Please note that excerpts and passages in the StudySync® library and this workbook are intended as touchstones to generate interest in an author's work. The excerpts and passages do not substitute for the reading of entire texts, and StudySync® strongly recommends that students seek out and purchase the whole literary or informational work in order to experience it as the author intended. Links to online resellers are available in our digital library. In addition, complete works may be ordered through an authorized reseller by filling out and returning to StudySync® the order form enclosed in this workbook.

Reading & Writing Companion   9

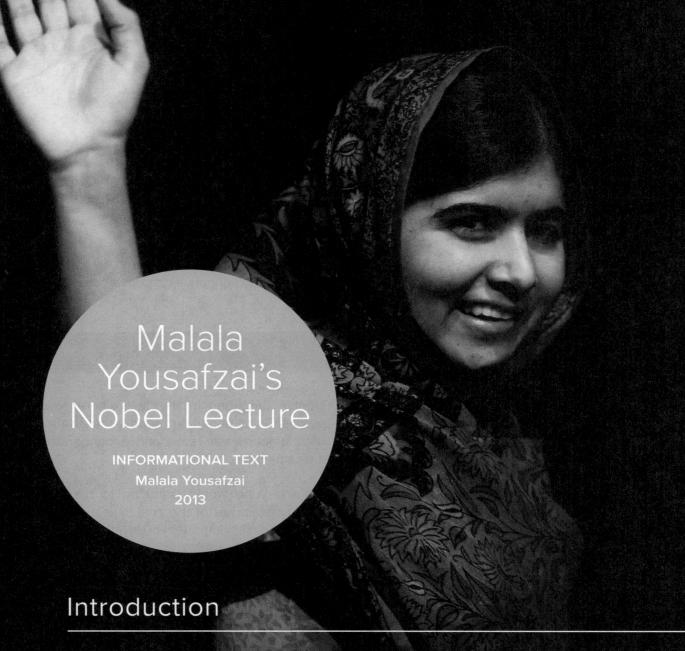

Malala Yousafzai's Nobel Lecture

INFORMATIONAL TEXT
Malala Yousafzai
2013

Introduction

The 2014 Nobel Peace Prize was awarded to two advocates for children's rights, one of them a Pakistani teenager named Malala Yousafzai. At seventeen, Malala was the youngest Nobel laureate in history. Malala had captured the world's attention two years earlier when a Taliban gunman shot her at close range as she was on her way home from school. She was targeted because she had long been speaking out against the Taliban's policy of forbidding education for girls; in fact, the Taliban had been bombing schools to make their point. In her Nobel Prize acceptance speech, Malala delivers a passionate rebuke to the Taliban's brutal anti-education policy and lays out her mission to promote a worldwide commitment to guaranteeing education for all children, surmounting the barriers of poverty, child labor, social taboos, and terrorist bullying.

"I had two options. One was to remain silent and wait to be killed. And the second was to speak up and then be killed."

1   *Bismillah hir rahman ir rahim. In the name of God, the most merciful, the most beneficent.*

2   Your Majesties, Your royal highnesses, distinguished members of the Norwegian Nobel Committee,

3   Dear sisters and brothers, today is a day of great happiness for me. I am humbled that the Nobel Committee has selected me for this precious award.

4   Thank you to everyone for your continued support and love. Thank you for the letters and cards that I still receive from all around the world. Your kind and encouraging words strengthens and inspires me.

5   I would like to thank my parents for their **unconditional** love. Thank you to my father for not clipping my wings and for letting me fly. Thank you to my mother for inspiring me to be patient and to always speak the truth — which we strongly believe is the true message of Islam. And also thank you to all my wonderful teachers, who inspired me to believe in myself and be brave.

6   I am proud, well in fact, I am very proud to be the first Pashtun, the first Pakistani, and the youngest person to receive this award. Along with that, along with that, I am pretty certain that I am also the first recipient of the Nobel Peace Prize who still fights with her younger brothers. I want there to be peace everywhere, but my brothers and I are still working on that.

7   I am also honoured to receive this award together with Kailash Satyarthi, who has been a champion for children's rights for a long time. Twice as long, in fact, than I have been alive. I am proud that we can work together, we can work together and show the world that an Indian and a Pakistani, they can work together and achieve their goals of children's rights.

8   Dear brothers and sisters, I was named after the inspirational Malalai of Maiwand who is the Pashtun Joan of Arc. The word Malala means "grief stricken", "sad", but in order to lend some happiness to it, my grandfather

would always call me Malala — "The happiest girl in the world" and today I am very happy that we are together fighting for an important cause.

9   This award is not just for me. It is for those forgotten children who want education. It is for those frightened children who want peace. It is for those voiceless children who want change.

10   I am here to stand up for their rights, to raise their voice. . . it is not time to pity them. It is not time to pity them. It is time to take action so it becomes the last time, the last time, so it becomes the last time that we see a child **deprived** of education.

11   I have found that people describe me in many different ways.

12   Some people call me the girl who was shot by the Taliban.

13   And some, the girl who fought for her rights.

14   Some people, call me a "Nobel Laureate" now.

15   However, my brothers still call me that annoying bossy sister. As far as I know, I am just a committed and even stubborn person who wants to see every child getting quality education, who wants to see women having equal rights and who wants peace in every corner of the world.

16   Education is one of the blessings of life — and one of its necessities. That has been my experience during the 17 years of my life. In my paradise home, Swat, I always loved learning and discovering new things. I remember when my friends and I would decorate our hands with henna[1] on special occasions. And instead of drawing flowers and patterns we would paint our hands with mathematical formulas and equations.

17   We had a thirst for education, we had a thirst for education because our future was right there in that classroom. We would sit and learn and read together. We loved to wear neat and tidy school uniforms and we would sit there with big dreams in our eyes. We wanted to make our parents proud and prove that we could also excel in our studies and achieve those goals, which some people think only boys can.

18   But things did not remain the same. When I was in Swat, which was a place of tourism and beauty, suddenly changed into a place of terrorism. I was just ten that more than 400 schools were destroyed. Women were flogged. People were killed. And our beautiful dreams turned into nightmares.

---

1. **henna** dye from the henna tree and/or the practice of making designs on the skin with it

Skill:
Informational
Text Structure

Malala first lists how others describe her. Then, she contrasts this list using "However," saying how her brothers describe her. Malala's description of herself is different from the rest because she says what she believes in. This is a compare and contrast text structure.

19   Education went from being a right to being a crime.

20   Girls were stopped from going to school.

21   When my world suddenly changed, my priorities changed too.

22   I had two options. One was to remain silent and wait to be killed. And the second was to speak up and then be killed.

23   I chose the second one. I decided to speak up.

24   We could not just stand by and see those injustices of the terrorists denying our rights, ruthlessly killing people and misusing the name of Islam. We decided to raise our voice and tell them: Have you not learnt, have you not learnt that in the Holy Quran[2] Allah says: if you kill one person it is as if you kill the whole **humanity**?

25   Do you not know that Mohammad, peace be upon him, the prophet of mercy, he says, do not harm yourself or others".

26   And do you not know that the very first word of the Holy Quran is the word "Iqra", which means "read"?

27   The terrorists tried to stop us and attacked me and my friends who are here today, on our school bus in 2012, but neither their ideas nor their bullets could win.

28   We survived. And since that day, our voices have grown louder and louder.

29   I tell my story, not because it is unique, but because it is not.

30   It is the story of many girls.

31   Today, I tell their stories too. I have brought with me some of my sisters from Pakistan, from Nigeria and from Syria, who share this story. My brave sisters Shazia and Kainat who were also shot that day on our school bus. But they have not stopped learning. And my brave sister Kainat Soomro who went through severe abuse and extreme violence, even her brother was killed, but she did not **succumb**.

32   Also my sisters here, whom I have met during my Malala Fund campaign. My 16-year-old courageous sister, Mezon from Syria, who now lives in Jordan as refugee and goes from tent to tent encouraging girls and boys to learn. And

2. **Quran** the primary sacred text of Islam

Skill:
Informational
Text Structure

Malala is using words like "suddenly changed" to show what happened after the terrorists took over her district. The sequential text structure helps me understand the order of events and why Malala took action.

Skill:
Media

Reading this part of the speech without watching and listening to Malala isn't the same. From the video, you can hear the audience begin to applaud her before she can finish her last sentence. The video shows the impact of her courage.

my sister Amina, from the North of Nigeria, where Boko Haram[3] threatens, and stops girls and even kidnaps girls, just for wanting to go to school.

33   Though I appear as one girl, though I appear as one girl, one person, who is 5 foot 2 inches tall, if you include my high heels. (It means I am 5 foot only) I am not a lone voice, I am not a lone voice, I am many.

34   I am Malala. But I am also Shazia.

35   I am Kainat.

36   I am Kainat Soomro.

37   I am Mezon.

38   I am Amina. I am those 66 million girls who are deprived of education. And today I am not raising my voice, it is the voice of those 66 million girls.

39   Sometimes people like to ask me why should girls go to school, why is it important for them. But I think the more important question is why shouldn't they, why shouldn't they have this right to go to school.

40   Dear sisters and brothers, today, in half of the world, we see rapid progress and development. However, there are many countries where millions still suffer from the very old problems of war, poverty, and injustice.

41   We still see conflicts in which innocent people lose their lives and children become orphans. We see many people becoming refugees in Syria, Gaza and Iraq. In Afghanistan, we see families being killed in suicide attacks and bomb blasts.

42   Many children in Africa do not have access to education because of poverty. And as I said, we still see, we still see girls who have no freedom to go to school in the north of Nigeria.

43   Many children in countries like Pakistan and India, as Kailash Satyarthi mentioned, many children, especially in India and Pakistan are deprived of their right to education because of social **taboos**, or they have been forced into child marriage or into child labour.

44   One of my very good school friends, the same age as me, who had always been a bold and confident girl, dreamed of becoming a doctor. But her dream remained a dream. At the age of 12, she was forced to get married. And then

---

3. **Boko Haram** Islamic jihadi group active in West Africa responsible for murders and kidnappings

soon she had a son, she had a child when she herself was still a child — only 14. I know that she could have been a very good doctor.

45 But she couldn't . . . because she was a girl.

46 Her story is why I dedicate the Nobel Peace Prize money to the Malala Fund, to help give girls quality education, everywhere, anywhere in the world and to raise their voices. The first place this funding will go to is where my heart is, to build schools in Pakistan — especially in my home of Swat and Shangla.

47 In my own village, there is still no secondary school for girls. And it is my wish and my commitment, and now my challenge to build one so that my friends and my sisters can go there to school and get quality education and to get this opportunity to fulfil their dreams.

48 This is where I will begin, but it is not where I will stop. I will continue this fight until I see every child, every child in school.

49 Dear brothers and sisters, great people, who brought change, like Martin Luther King and Nelson Mandela, Mother Teresa and Aung San Suu Kyi, once stood here on this stage. I hope the steps that Kailash Satyarthi and I have taken so far and will take on this journey will also bring change — lasting change.

50 My great hope is that this will be the last time, this will be the last time we must fight for education. Let's solve this once and for all.

51 We have already taken many steps. Now it is time to take a leap.

52 It is not time to tell the world leaders to realise how important education is — they already know it — their own children are in good schools. Now it is time to call them to take action for the rest of the world's children.

53 We ask the world leaders to unite and make education their top priority.

54 Fifteen years ago, the world leaders decided on a set of global goals, the Millennium Development Goals. In the years that have followed, we have seen some progress. The number of children out of school has been halved, as Kailash Satyarthi said. However, the world focused only on primary education, and progress did not reach everyone.

55 In year 2015, representatives from all around the world will meet in the United Nations to set the next set of goals, the **Sustainable** Development Goals. This will set the world's ambition for the next generations.

56 The world can no longer accept, the world can no longer accept that basic education is enough. Why do leaders accept that for children in developing countries, only basic literacy is sufficient, when their own children do homework in Algebra, Mathematics, Science and Physics?

57 Leaders must seize this opportunity to guarantee a free, quality, primary and secondary education for every child.

58 Some will say this is impractical, or too expensive, or too hard. Or maybe even impossible. But it is time the world thinks bigger.

59 Dear sisters and brothers, the so-called world of adults may understand it, but we children don't. Why is it that countries which we call strong" are so powerful in creating wars but are so weak in bringing peace? Why is it that giving guns is so easy but giving books is so hard? Why is it, why is it that making tanks is so easy, but building schools is so hard?

60 We are living in the modern age and we believe that nothing is impossible. We have reached the moon 45 years ago and maybe will soon land on Mars. Then, in this 21st century, we must be able to give every child quality education.

61 Dear sisters and brothers, dear fellow children, we must work. . . not wait. Not just the politicians and the world leaders, we all need to contribute. Me. You. We. It is our duty.

62 Let us become the first generation to decide to be the last, let us become the first generation that decides to be the last that sees empty classrooms, lost childhoods, and wasted potentials.

63 Let this be the last time that a girl or a boy spends their childhood in a factory.

64 Let this be the last time that a girl is forced into early child marriage.

65 Let this be the last time that a child loses life in war.

66 Let this be the last time that we see a child out of school.

67 Let this end with us.

68 Let's begin this ending . . . together . . . today . . . right here, right now. Let's begin this ending now.

69 Thank you so much.

© The Nobel Foundation 2014

First Read

Read "Malala Yousafzai - Nobel Lecture." After you read, complete the Think Questions below.

 THINK QUESTIONS

1. How does Malala feel about education? Cite textual evidence from the selection to support your answer.

2. What is the significance Malala places on the first word of the Quran?

3. Who are the "sisters" Malala describes? What challenges do the "sisters" face? Support your answer with textual evidence.

4. The word **deprive** comes, in part, from the Latin root *de-*, which means "away" or "against," and the Latin *privus,* which means "individual" or "single." With this in mind, what do you think the word *deprive* means? Write your best definition here and explain how you arrived at its meaning.

5. Use context clues to determine the meaning of the word **succumb** as it is used in the text. Write your definition here and tell how you got it.

Please note that excerpts and passages in the StudySync® library and this workbook are intended as touchstones to generate interest in an author's work. The excerpts and passages do not substitute for the reading of entire texts, and StudySync® strongly recommends that students seek out and purchase the whole literary or informational work in order to experience it as the author intended. Links to online resellers are available in our digital library. In addition, complete works may be ordered through an authorized reseller by filling out and returning to StudySync® the order form enclosed in this workbook.

Reading & Writing Companion **17**

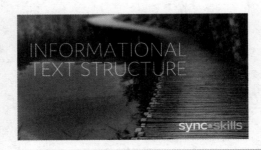

Skill:
Informational Text Structure

Use the Checklist to analyze Informational Text Structure in "Malala Yousafzai - Nobel Lecture." Refer to the sample student annotations about Informational Text Structure in the text.

••• CHECKLIST FOR INFORMATIONAL TEXT STRUCTURE

In order to determine the overall structure of a text, note the following:

✓ the topic(s) and how the author organizes information about the topic(s)

✓ patterns in a paragraph or section of text that reveal the text structure, such as:

- sequences, including the order of events or steps in a process

- problems and their solutions

- cause-and-effect relationships

- comparisons

✓ the overall structure of the text and how each section contributes to the development of ideas

To analyze how a particular sentence, paragraph, chapter, or section fits into the overall structure of a text and contributes to the development of the ideas, use the following questions as a guide:

✓ What organizational patterns reveal the text structure the author uses to present information?

✓ How does a particular sentence, paragraph, or section fit into the overall structure of the text? How does it affect the development of the author's ideas?

✓ In what ways does the text structure contribute to the development of ideas in the text?

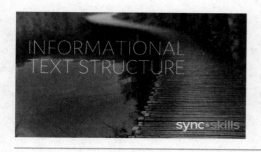

Skill:
Informational Text Structure

Reread paragraphs 27–38 from "Malala Yousafzai - Nobel Lecture." Then, using the Checklist on the previous page, answer the multiple-choice questions below.

YOUR TURN

1. Which informational text structure is used in paragraph 28?

   ○ A. compare and contrast
   ○ B. cause and effect
   ○ C. problem and solution
   ○ D. advantage and disadvantage

2. How does the pattern of saying "I am" in paragraphs 34–38 contribute to the development of ideas in the speech?

   ○ A. It shows that all of those girls have been shot.
   ○ B. It shows that all of those girls were forced to flee their countries.
   ○ C. It shows that Malala stands up for all girls and their education.
   ○ D. It shows that all of those girls have been kidnapped.

Please note that excerpts and passages in the StudySync® library and this workbook are intended as touchstones to generate interest in an author's work. The excerpts and passages do not substitute for the reading of entire texts, and StudySync® strongly recommends that students seek out and purchase the whole literary or informational work in order to experience it as the author intended. Links to online resellers are available in our digital library. In addition, complete works may be ordered through an authorized reseller by filling out and returning to StudySync® the order form enclosed in this workbook.

Reading & Writing
Companion   **19**

Skill:
Media

Use the Checklist to analyze Media in "Malala Yousafzai's Nobel Lecture." Refer to the sample student annotations about Media in the text.

••• CHECKLIST FOR MEDIA

In order to determine how information is presented in different media or formats, note the following:

- ✓ how the same topic can be treated, or presented, in more than one medium, including visual and audio

- ✓ how treatments of a topic through different kinds of media can give you more information about the topic

- ✓ details that are emphasized or missing in each medium and the reasons behind these choices

- ✓ how, if different details are stressed by different media, a reader or viewer may begin to think about the subject in a new way

To integrate information presented in different media or formats, consider the following questions:

- ✓ Which details are missing or emphasized in each medium? What do you think are the reasons behind these choices, and what effect do they have?

- ✓ What information can you learn by analyzing and comparing these two sources?

- ✓ How can you integrate the information presented in different media or formats?

- ✓ How does integrating information from different media and formats help you to develop a fuller and more coherent understanding of a topic?

Skill:
Media

Analyze characteristics of digital text in the following video clips from "Media." Then, using the Checklist on the previous page, answer the multiple-choice questions below.

⟳ YOUR TURN

1. Which of the following best describes how the video enhances the audio, and therefore, the watcher/listener's comprehension of this part of the speech?

   ○ A. The video shows how Malala's body language emphasizes what she is saying

   ○ B. The video shows a close-up of how people in the audience react to her speech

   ○ C. The video reveals the facial expressions of various committee members.

   ○ D. The video shows a contrast between Malala's gestures and her quiet voice.

2. What information communicated in this audio/visual clip would add to the text of Malala's speech?

   ○ A. The audio gives details about the girls, which makes their stories more important.

   ○ B. The video shows the girls who are named in Malala's speech.

   ○ C. The video and audio replicate the same information that is in the text without adding any details.

   ○ D. The video and audio give the girls' stories greater impact by showing who they are and telling what happened to them.

Please note that excerpts and passages in the StudySync® library and this workbook are intended as touchstones to generate interest in an author's work. The excerpts and passages do not substitute for the reading of entire texts, and StudySync® strongly recommends that students seek out and purchase the whole literary or informational work in order to experience it as the author intended. Links to online resellers are available in our digital library. In addition, complete works may be ordered through an authorized reseller by filling out and returning to StudySync® the order form enclosed in this workbook.

Reading & Writing Companion   21

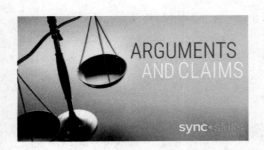

Skill:
Arguments and Claims

Use the Checklist to analyze Arguments and Claims in "Malala Yousafzai - Nobel Lecture." Refer to the sample student annotations about Arguments and Claims in the text.

••• CHECKLIST FOR ARGUMENTS AND CLAIMS

In order to trace the argument and specific claims, do the following:

✓ identify clues that reveal the speaker's opinion in the title, opening remarks, or concluding statement

✓ note the first and last sentence of each body paragraph for specific claims that help to build the speaker's argument

✓ listen for declarative statements that come before or follow an anecdote or story

✓ list the information that the speaker introduces in sequential order

✓ use different colored highlights to distinguish the speaker's argument, claims, reasoning, and evidence

✓ describe the speaker's argument in your own words

To evaluate the argument and specific claims, consider the following questions:

✓ Does the speaker support each claim with reasoning and evidence?

✓ In what order does the speaker introduce arguments and claims?

✓ Am I able to distinguish claims that are supported by reasoning and evidence from those that are not?

✓ Do the speaker's claims work together to support her overall argument?

✓ Which claims are not supported, if any?

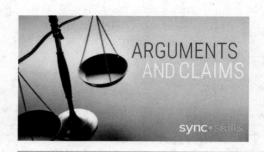

Skill:
Arguments and Claims

Reread paragraphs 57–61 and listen to 23:31–26:16 in the video of the speech of "Malala Yousafzai - Nobel Lecture." Then, using the Checklist on the previous page, answer the multiple-choice questions below.

↻ YOUR TURN

1. This question has two parts. First, answer Part A. Then, answer Part B.

Part A: Which of the following most closely reflects the argument of this section of the speech?

- ○ A. It is up to regular people to make sure all children have access to education.
- ○ B. All children deserve access to education regardless of where they live.
- ○ C. It is up to everybody to work together to make sure all children have access to education.
- ○ D. It is up to world leaders to make sure all children have access to education.

Part B: Which of following claims from the speech does NOT specifically contribute to the argument identified in Part A?

- ○ A. "Leaders must seize this opportunity to guarantee a free, quality, primary and secondary education for every child."
- ○ B. "We have reached the moon 45 years ago and maybe will soon land on Mars."
- ○ C. "Then, in this 21st century, we must be able to give every child quality education."
- ○ D. "Not just the politicians and the world leaders, we all need to contribute."

Please note that excerpts and passages in the StudySync® library and this workbook are intended as touchstones to generate interest in an author's work. The excerpts and passages do not substitute for the reading of entire texts, and StudySync® strongly recommends that students seek out and purchase the whole literary or informational work in order to experience it as the author intended. Links to online resellers are available in our digital library. In addition, complete works may be ordered through an authorized reseller by filling out and returning to StudySync® the order form enclosed in this workbook.

Reading & Writing Companion   **23**

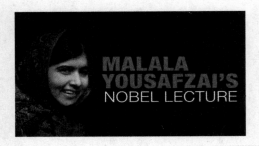

Close Read

Reread "Malala Yousafzai- Nobel Lecture." As you reread, complete the Skills Focus questions below. Then use your answers and annotations from the questions to help you complete the Write activity.

◎ SKILLS FOCUS

1. Identify places where Malala uses a cause and effect text structure to present information. Identify details or signal words that reveal the text structure.

2. Malala uses a variety of text structures in her speech. Identify places in the speech where she employs text structures other than cause and effect to get her message across. Explain how you determined the text structures.

3. Having experienced "Malala Yousafzai - Nobel Lecture" as a mixed-media presentation, identify and explain passages of the speech in which audio or video contributes to the meaning of Malala's words.

4. The Nobel Committee identified qualities in Malala that they believed made her worthy of receiving the Nobel Peace Prize in 2014. Identify evidence in the speech that illustrates qualities of character that help Malala in her efforts to promote education for all. Explain why you think these qualities matter.

✏ WRITE

ARGUMENTATIVE: Near the end of her speech, Malala gives a call to action. She says, "Dear sisters and brothers, dear fellow children, we must work . . . not wait. Not just the politicians and the world leaders, we all need to contribute. Me. You. We. It is our duty." Malala uses a combination of informational text structures in the course of her speech to communicate the idea contained in this call to action. Which do you think is the most effective, and why? Write a response using specific examples from the text and the video to support your claims.

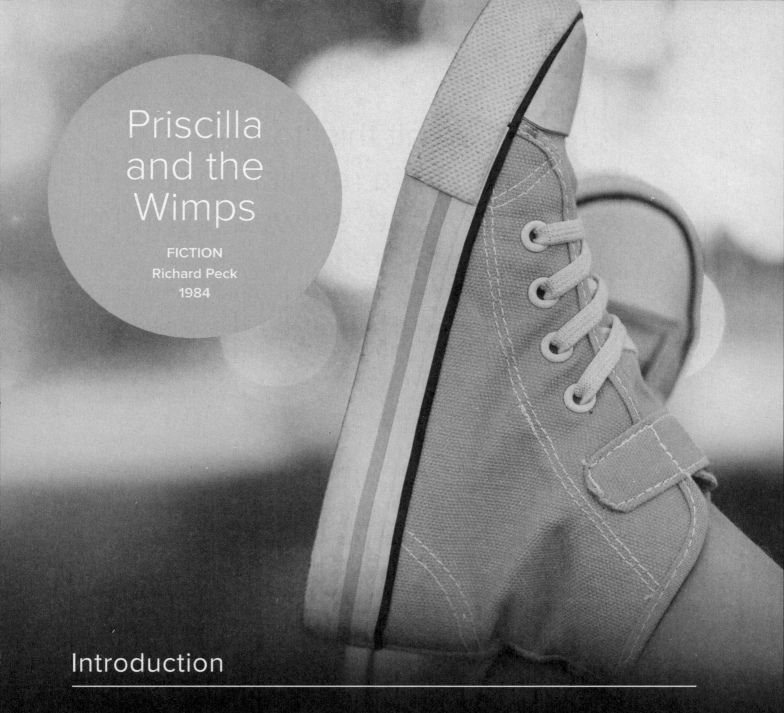

Priscilla and the Wimps

FICTION
Richard Peck
1984

Introduction

Richard Peck (b. 1934) is a Newbery Award-winning author who has written more than a dozen young adult novels in a prolific career spanning five decades. Peck first worked as a middle school teacher before his writing career began. He has said that his experiences with students inspired many of the characters and situations within his young adult books. In his story "Priscilla and the Wimps," Peck paints a vivid portrait of a school being ruled by a bully named Monk Klutter and his gang, known as Klutter's Kobras. Monk thinks he has the entire school under his thumb until he runs into someone even bigger than him—a girl named Priscilla Roseberry.

"I admit this, too:
I paid up on a regular basis.
And I might add: so would you."

1 Listen, there was a time when you couldn't even go to the *rest room* in this school without a pass. And I'm not talking about those little pink tickets made out by some teacher. I'm talking about a pass that could cost anywhere up to a buck, sold by Monk Klutter.

2 Not that Mighty Monk ever touched money, not in public. The gang he ran, which ran the school for him, was his collection agency. They were Klutter's Kobras, a name spelled out in nailheads on six well-known black plastic windbreakers.

3 Monk's threads were more . . . **subtle.** A pile-lined suede battle jacket with lizard-skin flaps over tailored Levis and a pair of ostrich-skin boots, brassed-toed and suitable for kicking people around. One of his Kobras did nothing all day but walk a half step behind Monk, carrying a fitted bag with Monk's gym shoes, a roll of restroom passes, a cashbox, and a switchblade that Monk gave himself manicures with at lunch over at the Kobras' table.

4 Speaking of lunch, there were a few cases of advanced malnutrition among the newer kids. The ones who were a little slow in handing over a cut of their lunch money and were therefore barred from the cafeteria. Monk ran a tight ship.

5 I admit it. I'm five foot five, and when the Kobras slithered by, with or without Monk, I shrank. I admit this, too: I paid up on a regular basis. And I might add: so would you.

6 This school was old Monk's Garden of Eden. Unfortunately for him, there was a serpent in it. The reason Monk didn't recognize trouble when it was staring him in the face is that the serpent in the Kobras' Eden was a girl.

7 Practically every guy in school could show you his scars. Fang marks from Kobras, you might say. And they were all highly **visible** in the shower room: lumps, lacerations, blue bruises, you name it. But girls usually got off with a warning.

8 Except there was this one girl named Priscilla Roseberry. Picture a girl named Priscilla Roseberry, and you'll be light years off. Priscilla was, hands down, the largest student in our particular institution of learning. I'm not talking fat. I'm talking big. Even beautiful, in a bionic way. Priscilla wasn't **inclined** toward organized crime. Otherwise, she could have put together a gang that would turn Klutter's Kobras into garter snakes.

9 Priscilla was basically a loner except she had one friend. A little guy named Melvin Detweiler. You talk about The Odd Couple. Melvin's one of the smallest guys above midget status ever seen. A really nice guy, but, you know—little. They even had lockers next to each other, in the same bank as mine. I don't know what they had going. I'm not saying this was a romance. After all, people deserve their privacy.

10 Priscilla was sort of above everything, if you'll pardon the pun. And very calm, as only the very big can be. If there was anybody who didn't notice Klutter's Kobras, it was Priscilla.

11 Until one winter day after school when we were all grabbing our coats out of our lockers. And hurrying, since Klutter's Kobras made sweeps of the halls for after-school shakedowns.

12 Anyway, up to Melvin's locker swaggers one of the Kobras. Never mind his name. Gang members don't need names. They've got group identity. He reaches down and grabs little Melvin by the neck and slams his head against his locker door. The sound of skull against steel rippled all the way down the locker row, speeding the crowds on their way.

13 "Okay, let's see your pass," snarls the Kobra.

14 "A pass for what this time?" Melvin asks, probably still dazed.

15 "Let's call it a pass for very short people," says the Kobra, "a dwarf tax." He wheezes a little Kobra chuckle at his own wittiness. And already he's reaching for Melvin's wallet with the hand that isn't circling Melvin's windpipe. All this time, of course, Melvin and the Kobra are standing in Priscilla's big shadow.

16 She's taking her time shoving her books into her locker and pulling on a very large-size coat. Then, quicker than the eye, she brings the side of her **enormous** hand down in a chop that breaks the Kobra's hold on Melvin's throat. You could hear a pin drop in that hallway. Nobody'd ever laid a finger on a Kobra, let alone a hand the size of Priscilla's.

17 Then Priscilla, who hardly ever says anything to anybody except Melvin, says to the Kobra, "Who's your leader, wimp?" This practically blows the Kobra

away. First he's chopped by a girl, and now she's acting like she doesn't know Monk Klutter, the Head Honcho of the World. He's so amazed, he tells her. "Monk Klutter."

18   "Never heard of him," Priscilla mentions. "Send him to see me." The Kobra just backs away from her like the whole **situation** is too big for him, which it is.

19   Pretty soon Monk himself slides up. He jerks his head once, and his Kobras slither off down the hall. He's going to handle this interesting case personally. "Who is it around here doesn't know Monk Klutter?"

20   He's standing inches from Priscilla, but since he'd have to look up at her, he doesn't. "Never heard of him," says Priscilla. Monk's not happy with this answer, but by now he's spotted Melvin, who's grown smaller in spite of himself. Monk breaks his own rule by reaching for Melvin with his own hands. "Kid," he says, "you're going to have to educate your girl friend."

21   His hands never quite make it to Melvin. In a move of pure poetry Priscilla has Monk in a hammerlock. His neck's popping like gunfire, and his head's bowed under the immense weight of her forearm. His suede jacket's peeling back, showing pile.

22   Priscilla's behind him in another easy motion. And with a single mighty thrust forward, frog-marches Monk into her own locker. It's incredible. His ostrich-skin boots click once in the air. And suddenly he's gone, neatly wedged into the locker, a perfect fit. Priscilla bangs the door shut, twirls the lock, and strolls out of school. Melvin goes with her, of course, trotting along below her shoulder. The last stragglers leave quietly.

23   Well, this is where fate, an even bigger force than Priscilla, steps in. It snows all that night, a blizzard. The whole town ices up. And school closes for a week.

"Priscilla and the Wimps" by Richard Peck from Sixteen: Short Stories by Outstanding Writers for Young Adults edited by Donald R. Gallo. Copyright © 1984. Used with permission of New York: Dell Publishing Company, Inc.

WRITE

PERSONAL RESPONSE: Write about a time that you have seen someone stand up to a bully or a threat, similar to the way Priscilla confronts Monk and the Kobras. In your response, compare the situation, the confrontation, and the result after the bully or threat was challenged.

Please note that excerpts and passages in the StudySync® library and this workbook are intended as touchstones to generate interest in an author's work. The excerpts and passages do not substitute for the reading of entire texts, and StudySync® strongly recommends that students seek out and purchase the whole literary or informational work in order to experience it as the author intended. Links to online resellers are available in our digital library. In addition, complete works may be ordered through an authorized reseller by filling out and returning to StudySync® the order form enclosed in this workbook.

Reading & Writing Companion 29

All Summer in a Day

FICTION
Ray Bradbury
1954

Introduction

Ray Bradbury (1920–2012) was an American writer best known for his works of science fiction. In Bradbury's short story "All Summer in a Day," the inhabitants of Venus live underground to avoid falling victim to the constant onslaught of rain. Only once every seven years does the rain stop and the sun comes out. Set in an elementary school classroom, a group of children await the sun's arrival. Only one of the kids, a girl named Margot who spent the first four years of her life on Earth, recalls the appearance of the sun. Rather than appreciating her knowledge,

"I think the sun is a flower, That blooms for just one hour."

NOTES

1   "Ready?"

2   "Ready."

3   "Now?"

4   "Soon."

5   "Do the scientists really know? Will it happen today, will it?"

6   "Look, look; see for yourself!"

7   The children pressed to each other like so many roses, so many weeds, intermixed, peering out for a look at the hidden sun.

8   It rained.

9   It had been raining for seven years; thousands upon thousands of days compounded and filled from one end to the other with rain, with the drum and gush of water, with the sweet crystal fall of showers and the concussion[1] of storms so heavy they were tidal waves come over the islands. A thousand forests had been crushed under the rain and grown up a thousand times to be crushed again. And this was the way life was forever on the planet Venus, and this was the schoolroom of the children of the rocket men and women who had come to a raining world to set up civilization and live out their lives.

10   "It's stopping, it's stopping!"

11   "Yes, yes!"

12   Margot stood apart from them, from these children who could not ever remember a time when there wasn't rain and rain and rain. They were all nine years old, and if there had been a day, seven years ago, when the sun came out for an hour and showed its face to the stunned world, they could not

---

1. **concussion** a brain injury caused by sudden impact

Skill:
Point of View

The narrator uses a character's name and the pronouns they and she, and seems to stand outside the story. The narrator also knows what Margot and the other children feel and think. Therefore, the point of view must be omniscient. The narrator is not a character in the story.

recall. Sometimes, at night, she heard them stir, in remembrance, and she knew they were dreaming and remembering gold or a yellow crayon or a coin large enough to buy the world with. She knew they thought they remembered a warmness, like a blushing in the face, in the body, in the arms and legs and trembling hands. But then they always awoke to the tatting drum, the endless shaking down of clear bead necklaces upon the roof, the walk, the gardens, the forests, and their dreams were gone.

13   All day yesterday they had read in class about the sun. About how like a lemon it was, and how hot. And they had written small stories or essays or poems about it: I think the sun is a flower, That blooms for just one hour. That was Margot's poem, read in a quiet voice in the still classroom while the rain was falling outside.

14   "Aw, you didn't write that!" protested one of the boys.

15   "I did," said Margot. "I did."

16   "William!" said the teacher.

17   But that was yesterday. Now the rain was slackening, and the children were crushed in the great thick windows.

18   "Where's teacher?"

19   "She'll be back."

20   "She'd better hurry, we'll miss it!"

21   They turned on themselves, like a feverish wheel, all tumbling spokes. Margot stood alone. She was a very frail girl who looked as if she had been lost in the rain for years and the rain had washed out the blue from her eyes and the red from her mouth and the yellow from her hair. She was an old photograph dusted from an album, whitened away, and if she spoke at all her voice would be a ghost. Now she stood, separate, staring at the rain and the loud wet world beyond the huge glass.

22   "What're you looking at?" said William.

23   Margot said nothing.

24   "Speak when you're spoken to."

25   He gave her a shove. But she did not move; rather she let herself be moved only by him and nothing else. They edged away from her, they would not look at her. She felt them go away. And this was because she would play no games with them in the echoing tunnels of the underground city. If they tagged her and ran,

she stood blinking after them and did not follow. When the class sang songs about happiness and life and games her lips barely moved. Only when they sang about the sun and the summer did her lips move as she watched the drenched windows. And then, of course, the biggest crime of all was that she had come here only five years ago from Earth, and she remembered the sun and the way the sun was and the sky was when she was four in Ohio. And they, they had been on Venus all their lives, and they had been only two years old when last the sun came out and had long since forgotten the color and heat of it and the way it really was. But Margot remembered.

26 "It's like a penny," she said once, eyes closed.

27 "No it's not!" the children cried.

28 "It's like a fire," she said, "in the stove."

29 "You're lying, you don't remember!" cried the children.

30 But she remembered and stood quietly apart from all of them and watched the patterning windows. And once, a month ago, she had refused to shower in the school shower rooms, had clutched her hands to her ears and over her head, screaming the water mustn't touch her head. So after that, dimly, dimly, she sensed it, she was different and they knew her difference and kept away. There was talk that her father and mother were taking her back to Earth next year; it seemed **vital** to her that they do so, though it would mean the loss of thousands of dollars to her family. And so, the children hated her for all these reasons of big and little **consequence**. They hated her pale snow face, her waiting silence, her thinness, and her possible future.

31 "Get away!" The boy gave her another push. "What're you waiting for?"

32 Then, for the first time, she turned and looked at him. And what she was waiting for was in her eyes.

33 "Well, don't wait around here!" cried the boy **savagely**. "You won't see nothing!"

34 Her lips moved.

35 "Nothing!" he cried. "It was all a joke, wasn't it?" He turned to the other children. "Nothing's happening today. *Is* it?"

36 They all blinked at him and then, understanding, laughed and shook their heads.

37 "Nothing, nothing!"

Skill:
Point of View

An omniscient narrator allows Bradbury to get across both Margot's and the other children's feelings. I think he wants readers to think about why there is conflict, not just about how Margot feels.

38 "Oh, but," Margot whispered, her eyes helpless. "But this is the day, the scientists predict, they say, they *know*, the sun. . ."

39 "All a joke!" said the boy, and seized her roughly. "Hey, everyone, let's put her in a closet before the teacher comes!"

40 "No," said Margot, falling back.

41 They surged about her, caught her up and bore her, protesting, and then pleading, and then crying, back into a tunnel, a room, a closet, where they slammed and locked the door. They stood looking at the door and saw it tremble from her beating and throwing herself against it. They heard her muffled cries. Then, smiling, they turned and went out and back down the tunnel, just as the teacher arrived.

42 "Ready, children?" She glanced at her watch.

43 "Yes!" said everyone.

44 "Are we all here?"

45 "Yes!"

46 The rain slacked still more.

47 They crowded to the huge door.

48 The rain stopped.

49 It was as if, in the midst of a film concerning an avalanche, a tornado, a hurricane, a volcanic eruption, something had, first, gone wrong with the sound apparatus, thus muffling and finally cutting off all noise, all of the blasts and repercussions and thunders, and then, second, ripped the film from the projector and inserted in its place a beautiful tropical slide which did not move or tremor. The world ground to a standstill. The silence was so **immense** and unbelievable that you felt your ears had been stuffed or you had lost your hearing altogether. The children put their hands to their ears. They stood apart. The door slid back and the smell of the silent, waiting world came into them.

50 The sun came out.

51 It was the color of flaming bronze and it was very large. And the sky around it was a blazing blue tile color. And the jungle burned with sunlight as the children, released from their spell, rushed out, yelling into the springtime.

Skill: Media

The text emphasizes how silent it is once the rain stops. In the video, the children are silent, and there's music playing. We get to see how confused they are because we can see their faces. When I visualized the story, I hadn't considered that they would be confused.

Skill: Media

In the text, the sun is described in detail. In the video, there are close-ups of the children's faces as the sun peeks through. The video shows each child with a unique reaction. Like in the text, they scatter when the sun comes out.

52 "Now, don't go too far," called the teacher after them. "You've only two hours, you know. You wouldn't want to get caught out!"

53 But they were running and turning their faces up to the sky and feeling the sun on their cheeks like a warm iron; they were taking off their jackets and letting the sun burn their arms. "Oh, it's better than the sun lamps, isn't it?"

54 "Much, much better!"

55 They stopped running and stood in the great jungle that covered Venus, that grew and never stopped growing, tumultuously, even as you watched it. It was a nest of octopi, clustering up great arms of flesh-like weed, wavering, flowering in this brief spring. It was the color of rubber and ash, this jungle, from the many years without sun. It was the color of stones and white cheeses and ink, and it was the color of the moon.

56 The children lay out, laughing, on the jungle mattress, and heard it sigh and squeak under them **resilient** and alive. They ran among the trees, they slipped and fell, they pushed each other, they played hide and-seek and tag, but most of all they squinted at the sun until the tears ran down their faces; they put their hands up to that yellowness and that amazing blueness and they breathed of the fresh, fresh air and listened and listened to the silence which suspended them in a blessed sea of no sound and no motion. They looked at everything and savored everything. Then, wildly, like animals escaped from their caves, they ran and ran in shouting circles. They ran for an hour and did not stop running.

57 And then —

58 In the midst of their running one of the girls wailed.

59 Everyone stopped.

60 The girl, standing in the open, held out her hand.

61 "Oh, look, look," she said, trembling.

62 They came slowly to look at her opened palm. In the center of it, cupped and huge, was a single raindrop. She began to cry, looking at it. They glanced quietly at the sun.

63 "Oh. Oh."

64 A few cold drops fell on their noses and their cheeks and their mouths. The sun faded behind a stir of mist. A wind blew cold around them. They turned and started to walk back toward the underground house, their hands at their sides, their smiles vanishing away.

65 A boom of thunder startled them and like leaves before a new hurricane, they tumbled upon each other and ran. Lightning struck ten miles away, five miles away, a mile, a half mile. The sky darkened into midnight in a flash.

66 They stood in the doorway of the underground for a moment until it was raining hard. Then they closed the door and heard the gigantic sound of the rain falling in tons and avalanches, everywhere and forever.

67 "Will it be seven more years?"

68 "Yes. Seven." Then one of them gave a little cry.

69 "Margot!"

70 "What?"

71 "She's still in the closet where we locked her."

72 "Margot."

73 They stood as if someone had driven them, like so many stakes, into the floor. They looked at each other and then looked away. They glanced out at the world that was raining now and raining and raining steadily. They could not meet each other's glances. Their faces were solemn and pale. They looked at their hands and feet, their faces down.

74 "Margot."

75 One of the girls said, "Well. . .?"

76 No one moved.

77 "Go on," whispered the girl.

78 They walked slowly down the hall in the sound of cold rain. They turned through the doorway to the room in the sound of the storm and thunder, lightning on their faces, blue and terrible. They walked over to the closet door slowly and stood by it.

79 Behind the closet door was only silence.

80 They unlocked the door, even more slowly, and let Margot out.

Reprinted by permission of Don Congdon Associates, Inc. Copyright (c) 1954, renewed 1982 by Ray Bradbury.

First Read

Read "All Summer in a Day." After you read, complete the Think Questions below.

☁ THINK QUESTIONS

1. How does Bradbury describe the sun? Citing at least two descriptive passages that you find in the text, explain what the sun means to the characters in the story.

2. Based on the text, how has life on Venus affected Margot? Cite specific evidence from the text to support your answer.

3. How do the children react to seeing the sun? Cite specific evidence from the text to support your answer.

4. Use context to determine the meaning of the word **immense** as it is used in paragraph 49. In your own words, define *immense* and explain how you found its meaning.

5. Read the following dictionary entry:

   consequence
   con•se•quence \'kän(t)-sə-ˌkwen(t)s\ *noun*

   1. a result or effect of an action or condition
   2. importance or relevance
   3. a conclusion reached by a line of reasoning

   Which definition most closely matches the meaning of **consequence** as it is used in paragraph 30? Write the correct definition of *consequence* here and explain how you figured out the correct meaning.

Please note that excerpts and passages in the StudySync® library and this workbook are intended as touchstones to generate interest in an author's work. The excerpts and passages do not substitute for the reading of entire texts, and StudySync® strongly recommends that students seek out and purchase the whole literary or informational work in order to experience it as the author intended. Links to online resellers are available in our digital library. In addition, complete works may be ordered through an authorized reseller by filling out and returning to StudySync® the order form enclosed in this workbook.

Reading & Writing Companion   **37**

Skill:
Point of View

Use the Checklist to analyze Point of View in "All Summer in a Day." Refer to the sample student annotations about Point of View in the text.

••• CHECKLIST FOR POINT OF VIEW

In order to identify the point of view of the narrator or speaker in a text, note the following:

- ✓ the speaker or narrator

- ✓ how much the narrator or speaker knows and reveals

- ✓ what the narrator or speaker says or does that reveals how they feel about other characters and events in the poem or story

To explain how an author develops the point of view of the narrator or speaker in a text, consider the following questions:

- ✓ Is the narrator or speaker objective and honest? Or do they mislead the reader? How?

- ✓ What is the narrator's or the speaker's point of view?

  - Is the narrator or speaker "all-knowing"; i.e., omniscient?

  - Is the narrator or speaker limited to revealing the thoughts and feelings of just one character?

  - Are there multiple narrators or speakers telling the story?

  - Are there multiple narrators or speakers telling the story?

  - Is the narrator a character within the story or telling the story from the "outside"?

- ✓ How does the narrator or speaker reveal his or her thoughts about the events or about the other characters in the story or poem? How do his or her experiences or cultural background affect those thoughts?

Skill:
Point of View

Reread paragraphs 56–62 from "All Summer in a Day." Then, using the Checklist on the previous page, answer the multiple-choice questions below.

🔁 YOUR TURN

1. If the story were told from a limited point of view from the perspective of Margot, how might paragraphs 56–62 be different?

   ○ A. The narrator would describe how the other children feel about being out in the sun.
   ○ B. The narrator would not be able to describe how the children feel, but only what they do or say.
   ○ C. The children would have to use the pronoun / to explain their own feelings.
   ○ D. The narrator would be asking the reader what he or she thought about the scene.

2. The author uses an omniscient point of view to achieve which of the following purposes?

   ○ A. To allow readers to empathize with the girl who catches the raindrop in her hand.
   ○ B. To reveal to readers the emotions the children feel about the sun.
   ○ C. To show the weather through one child's perspective.
   ○ D. To show the resilient quality of the rain.

Please note that excerpts and passages in the StudySync® library and this workbook are intended as touchstones to generate interest in an author's work. The excerpts and passages do not substitute for the reading of entire texts, and StudySync® strongly recommends that students seek out and purchase the whole literary or informational work in order to experience it as the author intended. Links to online resellers are available in our digital library. In addition, complete works may be ordered through an authorized reseller by filling out and returning to StudySync® the order form enclosed in this workbook.

Reading & Writing Companion   39

Skill:
Theme

Use the Checklist to analyze Theme in "All Summer in a Day ." Refer to the sample student annotations about Theme in the text.

In order to *infer* a theme in a text, note the following:

- ✓ the topic of the text

- ✓ whether or not the theme is stated directly in the text

- ✓ details in the text that may reveal the theme

  - the title and chapter headings

  - details about the setting

  - a narrator's or speaker's tone

  - a narrator's or speaker's point of view

  - use of figurative language

  - characters' thoughts, actions, and dialogue

  - the central conflict in the story's plot

  - the resolution of the conflict

- ✓ analyze how characters and the problems they face are affected by the setting or events, and what impact this may have on how the theme is developed

To determine how a theme is conveyed through particular details, consider the following questions:

- ✓ What is the theme or central idea of the text?

- ✓ What details helped to reveal that theme?

- ✓ When did you become aware of that theme? For instance, did the story's conclusion reveal the theme?

Skill:
Theme

Reread paragraphs 13–15 of "Priscilla and the Wimps" and paragraphs 12–15 of "All Summer in a Day." Then, using the Checklist on the previous page, answer the multiple-choice questions below.

⟳ YOUR TURN

1. This question has two parts. First, answer Part A. Then, answer Part B.

Part A: From the excerpts above, the reader can infer that another theme across both texts is

- ○ A. Violence is not a successful way to solve problems.
- ○ B. People are often unkind toward those they perceive as different from themselves.
- ○ C. Sometimes people hide their fear by being mean to others.
- ○ D. It's better to avoid or hide from a bully than try to confront one.

Part B: The sentences from each text that best suggest this theme are —

- ○ A. From "Priscilla and the Wimps": "Okay, let's see your pass," snarls the Kobra. From "All Summer in a Day": "Aw, you didn't write that!" protested one of the boys.
- ○ B. From "Priscilla and the Wimps": He wheezes a little Kobra chuckle at his own wittiness. From "All Summer in a Day": That was Margot's poem, read in a quiet voice in the still classroom while the rain was falling outside.
- ○ C. From "Priscilla and the Wimps": "Let's call it a pass for very short people," says the Kobra, "a dwarf tax." From "All Summer in a Day": Margot stood apart from them, from these children who could not ever remember a time when there wasn't rain and rain and rain.
- ○ D. From "Priscilla and the Wimps": And already he's reaching for Melvin's wallet with the hand that isn't circling Melvin's windpipe. From "All Summer in a Day": But then they always awoke to the tatting drum, the endless shaking down of clear bead necklaces upon the roof, the walk, the gardens, the forests, and their dreams were gone.

Please note that excerpts and passages in the StudySync® library and this workbook are intended as touchstones to generate interest in an author's work. The excerpts and passages do not substitute for the reading of entire texts, and StudySync® strongly recommends that students seek out and purchase the whole literary or informational work in order to experience it as the author intended. Links to online resellers are available in our digital library. In addition, complete works may be ordered through an authorized reseller by filling out and returning to StudySync® the order form enclosed in this workbook.

Reading & Writing Companion   **41**

Skill:
Media

Use the Checklist to analyze Media in "All Summer in a Day." Refer to the sample student annotations about Media in the text.

••• CHECKLIST FOR MEDIA

In order to determine how to compare and contrast reading a story, drama, or poem to listening to or viewing an audio, video, or live version of a text, do the following:

- ✓ choose a story that has been presented in multiple forms of media, such as a written story and a film adaptation

- ✓ think about the key features of the different media presentations

- ✓ consider how different kinds of media treat story elements in different ways

- ✓ think about what you "see"—or visualize—as well as "hear" when you read a story, drama, or poem and how it compares to seeing it as a film, or hearing it read aloud

To compare and contrast the experience of reading a story, drama, or poem to listening to or viewing an audio, video, or live version of the text, including contrasts between what they "see" and "hear" as they are reading the text and what they perceive as they are listening or watching. Consider the following questions:

- ✓ What features of each medium are the most important?

- ✓ Do you listen to it or view it? Do you hear one voice or many? How do these affect the written work?

- ✓ How is the way you picture a character in your mind as you read similar to the way that same character is portrayed in a filmed version of the same story? How is it different?

Skill: Media

Reread paragraphs 53–56 from "All Summer in a Day." Then, using the Checklist on the previous page, answer the multiple-choice questions below.

⟳ YOUR TURN

1. What is the most significant difference between paragraphs 53-56 of the printed version and the video clip of the story "All Summer in a Day"?

   ○ A. The children speak in the story and they don't in the video clip.
   ○ B. The setting is different: the children are in a jungle in the story, but not in the video.
   ○ C. There are no differences.
   ○ D. The children don't lie down in the video, which they do in the text.

2. What is the most significant similarity between paragraphs 53-56 of the printed version and the video clip of the story "All Summer in a Day"?

   ○ A. Both versions emphasize that the sun is out.
   ○ B. Both versions emphasize how cruel the children are to Margot.
   ○ C. Both versions emphasize how excited the children are by having them run wildly.
   ○ D. They are not similar at all.

Please note that excerpts and passages in the StudySync® library and this workbook are intended as touchstones to generate interest in an author's work. The excerpts and passages do not substitute for the reading of entire texts, and StudySync® strongly recommends that students seek out and purchase the whole literary or informational work in order to experience it as the author intended. Links to online resellers are available in our digital library. In addition, complete works may be ordered through an authorized reseller by filling out and returning to StudySync® the order form enclosed in this workbook.

Reading & Writing Companion   **43**

Close Read

Reread "All Summer in a Day." As you reread, complete the Skills Focus questions below. Then use your answers and annotations from the questions to help you complete the Write activity.

◎ SKILLS FOCUS

1. Identify places in "All Summer in a Day" where an omniscient point of view helps the author to achieve a specific purpose.

2. Identify a theme that is common to both "Priscilla and the Wimps" and "All Summer in a Day." Support your answer with evidence from both texts.

3. Although the narrator occasionally addresses the reader, "Priscilla and the Wimps" is told from the point of view of a character within the story. Highlight a passage in "All Summer in a Day" that deals with bullying. Compare the effectiveness of the point of view in that passage with the effectiveness of the narrator's descriptions of bullying in "Priscilla and the Wimps."

4. Compare and contrast the scene in which the children experience the sun in "All Summer in a Day" in the printed text with the same scene in the video clip. Be sure to use textual evidence to support your response.

5. Identify evidence in "All Summer in a Day" that reveals how the children born on Venus change by the end of the story, and develop new character traits, or qualities. Explain what these new qualities are, what brings about the change, and why these new qualities are important.

✎ WRITE

COMPARATIVE: Compare and contrast the points of view in "Priscilla and the Wimps" and "All Summer in a Day." Explain how the point of view in each text illustrates important themes about bullying. In your response, be sure to cite evidence from both texts.

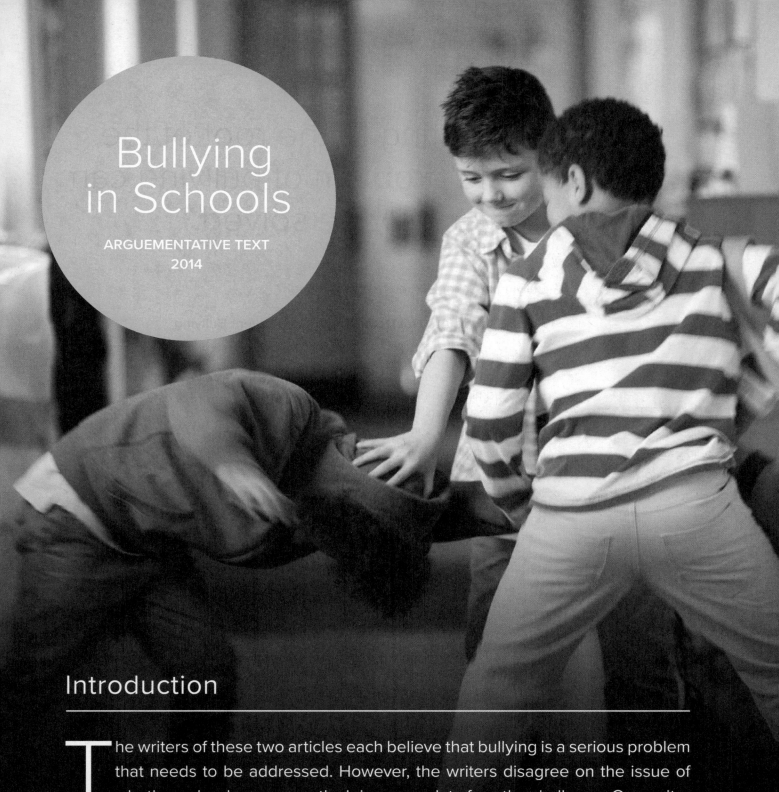

Bullying in Schools

ARGUEMENTATIVE TEXT
2014

Introduction

The writers of these two articles each believe that bullying is a serious problem that needs to be addressed. However, the writers disagree on the issue of whether schools are currently doing enough to face the challenge. One writer argues that schools have not invested nearly enough effort in creating safeguards and programs to protect students and prevent bullying. The other writer argues that most schools now take bullying very seriously and have initiated enough programs to address the problem effectively. Both writers present strong arguments and support their claims with evidence. Which argument do you feel is more convincing?

"Without getting to the root of the situation, the problem of bullying can never truly be solved."

NOTES

Bullying in Schools: Are we doing enough?

Point: Schools Are Not Doing Enough to Prevent Bullying

Skill: Arguments and Claims

The writer restates the claim made in the title and follows with reasons why not enough is being done. In the last sentence, the writer makes another claim to convince readers why bullying is such a serious and immediate problem.

Skill: Reasons and Evidence

The statistic cited in paragraph 2 is evidence that supports the claim the author makes in the first sentence of the paragraph.

---

1   Although the media continues to raise public awareness of student bullying, many schools are still not doing enough to solve the problem. Most teachers and school administrators do not witness bullying. Sometimes they don't know how to recognize it. Sometimes they ignore it. They may also hold the age-old attitude that bullying is just something children do or go through. They think it's a normal part of growing up. But we know now that the **repercussions** of bullying can be lasting and **severe.** Sometimes they even end in tragedy.

2   The fact that a huge amount of bullying still happens demonstrates that not enough is being done about the issue. The exact number of victims is hard to determine because many incidents go unreported. The National Center for Education Statistics reported in 2013 that one of three students is bullied either in school or through social media. This statistic includes both physical and emotional harassment. Either form can leave lasting scars on victims. Students who are bullied often become very stressed. They can have trouble sleeping and begin to do poorly in school. Furthermore, victims are at a greater risk of suffering from low self-esteem, anxiety, and depression. These effects can even continue well into adulthood.

3   One way in which schools are failing to keep pace with the problem is in adequately supervising school property. Bullying usually happens in unsupervised areas like bathrooms, cafeterias, and school buses. The simplest solution would be for schools to put teachers, monitors, or aides in these areas. Unfortunately, many schools do not have enough staff to ensure that these areas are supervised.

4   An even harder venue to monitor for bullying is the Internet. Cyber-bullying, or bullying that happens over social media, is often extremely hard to track. It is easy to delete comments or pictures before authority figures can see them. In many cases there is little evidence to go on. Students, teachers, and administrators all need to be educated about how to deal with the challenge

---

 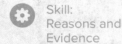

of cyber-bullying. There are not currently enough programs that address this issue.

Cyber-bulling can be hard for schools to monitor.

5   Most schools also do not have a clear procedure or policy for investigating bullying. This means that if a victim is brave enough to come forward and ask for help, he or she often does not receive it. This is because administrators and authorities do not have a set path for examining the situation. They do not have a plan for ending harmful situations.

6   In addition to educating teachers and administrators about bullying, schools need more programs to help students themselves address the problem. Top-down approaches that simply dole out punishments for bullies are not enough to solve the problem. Students need to be taught more about the ways their words and actions can hurt others. They also need to learn that cases of bullying are often more complex than a "perpetrator" and a "victim." Often, a situation of **perceived** "bullying" is actually made up of several smaller events. Different students may have played different roles. A student may be bullied one day and become the bully the next. These complicated interactions and behavior can make it difficult to find a solution that will satisfy all parties.

7   Many schools have "zero-**tolerance**" policies regarding bullying. These policies are often not sensitive enough to students' particular needs and reasons for behaving the way they do. Every school is different, and student issues can vary widely. Teachers and administrators need to listen carefully to students' problems and perceived injustices, and be sensitive to them. If a student is punished for being a bully when he or she has a different perspective on the situation, that student may feel unfairly persecuted or "ganged-up on." Casting bullies as one-sided villains can be just as damaging to a student as being bullied.

8   Another issue with these "zero-tolerance" policies is that they can often encourage teachers and administrators to over-discipline students. Sometimes one-time or casual conflicts between students can be blown out of proportion. Students may be punished needlessly.

9   We need more policies and programs in place to educate students, teachers, administrators, and parents about what bullying is and how to recognize it. Policies and programs need to show how to end bullying, and, most importantly, what *causes* it. Most schools that do have anti-bullying strategies only deal with the surface of the problem. They don't address the underlying causes. Without getting to the root of the situation, the problem of bullying can never truly be solved.

NOTES

Skill:
Arguments and Claims

The writer argues that programs and policies should be designed to help people understand fully what bullying is, why it happens, and how it can be stopped. He claims that existing anti-bullying strategies fail to go to the root of the problem, and until we understand what causes bullying the problem will remain unsolved.

Copyright © BookheadEd Learning, LLC

"Some of the effort needs to be made on the part of the parents."

Counterpoint: Most Schools Are Doing Their Best to Stop Bullying

10   A group of students is playing on the playground. One boy pokes another in the back while waiting in line for the swings. "Knock it off," says the boy. "That's not nice."

11   "Oh, sorry," says the first boy, and stops. "I didn't really mean that."

12   This is the sort of response you might hear on the playground at a school in Forest Lakes, Minnesota, where Dave Seaburg is a teacher. In many schools across the country, bullying is being reduced or eliminated thanks to anti-bullying programs and policies. These programs are carried out by dedicated teachers like Mr. Seaburg. As part of an anti-bullying program, he leads workshops and provides lessons designed to teach students about the harmful effects of bullying. Students also learn ways to empower themselves against it. The school district where Dave Seaburg works has seen a steady decline in bullying since anti-bullying programs were implemented.

13   Schools across the United States are in fact doing an enormous amount to meet the challenge of bullying. As the media has heightened awareness of the issue, the attention devoted to solving the problem has been growing steadily. One example would be schools in the state of New Jersey. The first law against bullying in New Jersey schools was passed by the state legislature a little more than a decade ago. Within a few years, school districts were required to appoint an anti-bullying coordinator in every school. Today, according to the *Asbury Park Press,* each New Jersey school district spends more than thirty thousand dollars a year on supplies, software, additional personnel, and staff and teacher training devoted to anti-bullying measures.

14   How many school districts are expending this kind of effort? Certainly, many hundreds. More than forty-five states currently have laws on the books that direct school districts to adopt anti-bullying programs. Organizations from the National Education Association to the National Association of Student Councils are developing initiatives aimed at preventing bullying.

15 What exactly do school programs to prevent bullying do, and how do they work? There is no one single profile. A New Hampshire law states that all school staff must be trained to know what bullying looks like. People learn to spot the signs, and those who see bullying must report it. In Midland, Texas, police officers visit the schools to let students know that bullying is a crime. A school district in Miami, Florida has implemented several anti-bullying programs including Challenge Day and Girls Day Out. Girls Day Out teaches girls how they can deal with social issues in a positive way rather than resorting to bullying.

16 When it comes to cyberbullying, it can be extremely difficult for a school to monitor and police students' activity on social media. Some of the effort needs to be made on the part of the parents. When parents take an active role in their children's social media usage, it becomes much easier to keep track of what's going on. Also, students are less likely to cyberbully if they know their Internet activity is being supervised and they are being held accountable for their actions. Even in the arena of cyberbullying, however, there is a role schools can and do play. In more than a dozen states, schools have been authorized to take disciplinary action against students who engage in bullying that takes place off of school property.

17 For example, the state of California recently passed Seth's Law. This new law strengthens the anti-bullying legislation that is already in place. It requires all California public schools to regularly update their anti-bullying programs and policies. There are even provisions for cyber-bullying. Seth's Law also focuses on protecting students who are victims of bullying due to their race, gender, sexual orientation, religion, or disabilities. Seth's Law makes it mandatory for teachers and authority figures to take action against any bullying behavior that they witness.

18 If school anti-bullying programs vary widely, are there any general guidelines that can be recommended? Certainly controversial issues exist where school policies are concerned. Should bullies be suspended or otherwise punished, or should they be helped with counseling and anger management programs? Should bystanders who witness bullying and fail to report it be reprimanded? Should schools be involved at all, or is bullying a family matter, as some people contend?

19 The federal government hosts a website, http://stopbullying.gov, with information for students, parents, and teachers on the issue of bullying. It suggests a number of different measures that schools can implement. For teachers and staff, these measures include finding out why, when, and where bullying takes place; launching awareness campaigns; creating school safety committees; and building information into the student curriculum. The website

also recommends something that can be useful everywhere at all times—creating a culture of **civility** and tolerance.

20 Most schools are doing all they can to raise awareness, prevent, and ultimately eliminate bullying. If they devote any more time to anti-bullying education than they already do, it will take time away from core subjects like math and language arts. Anti-bullying programs are expensive for schools to run and they require highly trained staff.

21 Still, even with the very best anti-bullying programs and policies, it can take a long time for change to come about. It may be as many as three to ten years before an anti-bullying culture becomes standard all over the country. Though it may not seem like schools are doing enough because bullying still **persists**, even the most effective programs will take time to bring about the sort of change people are looking for.

First Read

Read "Bullying in Schools." After you read, complete the Think Questions below.

☁ THINK QUESTIONS

1. Use details from the text to explain the Point author's response to the issue of "Bullying in Schools." Cite the Point author's main claim and one reason why the author makes the claim. What evidence does the author use to support this position?

2. Use details from the text to explain the Counterpoint author's response to the issue of "Bullying in Schools." Cite the Counterpoint author's main claim and one reason why the author makes this claim. What evidence does the author use to support this position?

3. The Point author acknowledges that some schools have "zero-tolerance policies," but he or she is critical of them. Explain why the author criticizes these policies. Use textual evidence to support your answer.

4. Use context to determine the meaning of the word severe as it is used in "Point: Schools Are Not Doing Enough to Prevent Bullying." Write your definition of *severe* here and explain how you determined its meaning. Then, check your inferred definition both in context and with a dictionary.

5. The Latin root *per-* means "through or during" and the Latin *sistere* means "to stand." With this in mind, try to infer the meaning of the word **persists** as it is used in the final paragraph. Write your definition of *persists* here and explain how you determined its meaning.

Please note that excerpts and passages in the StudySync® library and this workbook are intended as touchstones to generate interest in an author's work. The excerpts and passages do not substitute for the reading of entire texts, and StudySync® strongly recommends that students seek out and purchase the whole literary or informational work in order to experience it as the author intended. Links to online resellers are available in our digital library. In addition, complete works may be ordered through an authorized reseller by filling out and returning to StudySync® the order form enclosed in this workbook.

Reading & Writing Companion

51

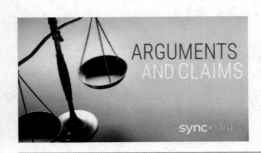

Skill:
Arguments and Claims

Use the Checklist to analyze Arguments and Claims in "Bullying in Schools." Refer to the sample student annotations about Arguments and Claims in the text.

••• CHECKLIST FOR ARGUMENTS AND CLAIMS

In order to trace the argument and specific claims, do the following:

- ✓ identify clues that reveal the author's opinion in the title, introduction, or conclusion

- ✓ note the first and last sentence of each body paragraph for specific claims that help to build the author's argument

- ✓ list the information that the writer introduces in sequential order

- ✓ use a different color highlight to distinguish the writer's argument, claims, reasoning, and evidence

- ✓ describe the speaker's argument in your own words

To evaluate the argument and specific claims, consider the following questions:

- ✓ Does the writer support each claim with reasoning and evidence?

- ✓ Am I able to distinguish claims that are supported by reasons and evidence from those that are not?

- ✓ Do the writer's claims work together to support the writer's overall argument?

- ✓ Which claims are not supported, if any?

Skill:
Arguments and Claims

Reread paragraphs 13, 16, and 21 of the second writer's Counterpoint from "Bullying in Schools." Then, using the Checklist on the previous page, answer the multiple-choice questions below.

⟳ YOUR TURN

1. What claim does the writer make about the topic in paragraph 13?

   ○ A. The media is focusing on the issue of bullying.

   ○ B. Schools are making a big effort to meet the challenge of bullying.

   ○ C. Anti-bullying programs have been in schools for more than ten years.

   ○ D. New Jersey spends a lot of time and money on anti-bullying programs.

2. In paragraph 16, what claim does the writer make about addressing cyberbullying?

   ○ A. Parents need to be involved in monitoring social media usage.

   ○ B. Social media usage cannot be monitored.

   ○ C. Students will not cyberbully if Internet usage is supervised.

   ○ D. Schools cannot discipline bullying off school property.

3. In the conclusion of the counterpoint, in paragraph 21, what does the writer want readers to believe?

   ○ A. Effective bullying programs in schools are rare, even after ten years.

   ○ B. Bullying will persist no matter how effective programs are.

   ○ C. The best anti-bullying programs take effect in a short time.

   ○ D. It takes a long time for anti-bullying programs to work, so people need to be patient.

Please note that excerpts and passages in the StudySync® library and this workbook are intended as touchstones to generate interest in an author's work. The excerpts and passages do not substitute for the reading of entire texts, and StudySync® strongly recommends that students seek out and purchase the whole literary or informational work in order to experience it as the author intended. Links to online resellers are available in our digital library. In addition, complete works may be ordered through an authorized reseller by filling out and returning to StudySync® the order form enclosed in this workbook.

Reading & Writing Companion   53

Skill:
Reasons and Evidence

Use the Checklist to analyze Reasons and Evidence in "Bullying in Schools." Refer to the sample student annotations about Reasons and Evidence in the text.

••• CHECKLIST FOR REASONS AND EVIDENCE

In order to identify claims that are supported by reasons and evidence, do the following:

- ✓ look for the argument the author is making

- ✓ identify the claim or the main idea of the argument

- ✓ find the reasons and evidence that support the claim

To distinguish claims that are supported by reasons and evidence from claims that are not, consider the following questions:

- ✓ What reasons does the author give to support his claim?

- ✓ What kinds of evidence does the author include to support his or her reasons?

- ✓ Does each piece of evidence support the claim? Why or why not?

- ✓ Are there any claims that are not supported by reasons and evidence? If so, what kinds of reasons or evidence would the author need to include?

Skill:
Reasons and Evidence

Reread paragraphs 4–5 of the Counterpoint argument. from "Bullying in Schools." Then, using the Checklist on the previous page, answer the multiple-choice questions below.

↻ YOUR TURN

1. Which of the following best supports the claim that New Jersey is doing a lot to prevent bullying?

   ○ A. Every school must appoint an anti-bullying coordinator.
   ○ B. The news and media have covered the issue of bullying.
   ○ C. 45 states have created anti-bullying programs.
   ○ D. Teacher training for anti-bullying procedures are available.

2. Which of the following claims is NOT supported by evidence in the second paragraph of this passage?

   ○ A. Laws that attempt to prevent bullying in schools are in effect in many states.
   ○ B. New Jersey spends money each year on their anti-bullying platform.
   ○ C. There are extensive efforts being made in an attempt to prevent bullying.
   ○ D. Hundreds of other school districts are putting forth effort.

Please note that excerpts and passages in the StudySync® library and this workbook are intended as touchstones to generate interest in an author's work. The excerpts and passages do not substitute for the reading of entire texts, and StudySync® strongly recommends that students seek out and purchase the whole literary or informational work in order to experience it as the author intended. Links to online resellers are available in our digital library. In addition, complete works may be ordered through an authorized reseller by filling out and returning to StudySync® the order form enclosed in this workbook.

Reading & Writing Companion   55

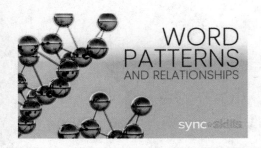

Skill: Word Patterns and Relationships

Use the Checklist to analyze Word Patterns and Relationships in "Bullying in Schools." Refer to the sample student annotations about Word Patterns and Relationships in the text.

••• CHECKLIST FOR WORD PATTERNS AND RELATIONSHIPS

In order to determine the relationship between particular words to better understand each of the words, note the following:

- ✓ any unfamiliar words in the text

- ✓ the surrounding words and phrases in order to better understand the meanings or possible relationships between words

- ✓ examples of part/whole, item/category, or other relationships between words, such as cause/effect, where what happens is a result of something

- ✓ the meaning of a word

To use the relationship between particular words to better understand each of the words, consider the following questions:

- ✓ Are these words related to each other in some way? How?

- ✓ What kind of relationship do these words have?

- ✓ Can any of these words be defined by using a part/whole, item/category, or cause/effect relationship?

Skill: Word Patterns and Relationships

Reread paragraphs 7–8 of the Counterpoint article in "Bullying in Schools." Then, using the Checklist on the previous page, answer the multiple-choice questions below.

⟳ YOUR TURN

1. In paragraph 7, the author explains that schools are allowed to take *disciplinary action* against bullies. Then, the author goes on to describe the intended results of *disciplinary action* in paragraph 8. This is an example of what kind of word relationship?

   ○ A. Word patterns

   ○ B. Cause/effect relationship

   ○ C. Part/whole relationship

   ○ D. Item/category relationship

2. How does recognizing the relationship between *disciplinary action* and the intended results help you to better understand the text?

   ○ A. The relationship between the term *disciplinary action* and the intended results allows the reader to understand the severity of cyberbullying and the necessity of prevention..

   ○ B. The relationship between *disciplinary action* and its intended results provides the reader with insight concerning how laws are made.

   ○ C. The relationship between *disciplinary action* and the intended results emphasizes the idea that there is not enough being done in school to prevent bullying.

   ○ D. The relationship between *disciplinary action* and the intended results highlights the understanding that schools don't have a bullying problem.

Close Read

Reread "Bullying in Schools." As you reread, complete the Skills Focus questions below. Then use your answers and annotations from the questions to help you complete the Write activity.

◎ SKILLS FOCUS

1. Identify evidence that supports the claim made in the Point argument that many schools are not doing enough to prevent bullying. Explain how the evidence supports the claim.

2. Identify the evidence the writer of the Counterpoint argument uses to support the claim that schools are doing a lot to meet the challenges of bullying. Then, identify claims that are not supported by reasons or evidence.

3. Identify evidence from the Point and Counterpoint arguments that claims students can be taught not to bully and to protect themselves from being bullied. Explain how the evidence relates to the Essential Question: Which qualities of character matter most?

✏ WRITE

DEBATE: Which of the two arguments do you consider to be more persuasive? As you prepare for your debate, use the graphic organizer to consider how the arguments develop and if you think their claims will convince the readers. After choosing a position, **justify** your claims by citing reasons and evidence from the text in the debate with your classmates. After your debate, you will write a reflection in the space below.

Freedom
Walkers:
The Story of the
Montgomery Bus Boycott

INFORMATIONAL TEXT
Russell Freedman
2006

Introduction

Rosa Parks's famous refusal to give up her seat on a Montgomery, Alabama bus was part of a planned civil action. Nine months earlier, fifteen-year-old Claudette Colvin spontaneously made the same decision, confronting a

"Claudette had been studying the U.S. Constitution and the Bill of Rights, and she had taken those lessons to heart."

Chapter 2: Claudette Colvin

1   *"It's my constitutional right!"*

2   Two youngsters from New Jersey-sixteen-year-old Edwina Johnson and her brother Marshall, who was fifteen-arrived in Montgomery to visit relatives during the summer of 1949. No one told them about the city's segregation laws for buses, and one day they boarded a bus and sat down by a white man and boy.

3   The white boy told Marshall to get up from the seat beside him. Marshall refused. Then the bus driver ordered the black teenagers to move, but they continued to sit where they were. Up North, they were accustomed to riding integrated buses and trains. They didn't see now why they should give up their seats.

4   The driver called the police, and Edwina and Marshall were arrested. Held in jail for two days, they were convicted at a court hearing of violating the city's segregation laws. Judge Wiley C. Hill threatened to send them to reform school until they were twenty-one, but relatives managed to get them an attorney. They were fined and sent back to New Jersey.

5   During the next few years, other black riders were arrested and convicted for the same offense-sitting in seats reserved for whites. They paid their fines quietly and continued to ride the public buses. It took a spunky fifteen-year-old high school student to bring matters to a head.

6   Claudette Colvin was an A student at all-black Booker T. Washington High. She must have been paying attention in her **civics** classes, for she insisted on applying the lessons she had learned after boarding a city bus on March 2, 1955.

7   Claudette was on her way home from school that day. She found a seat in the middle of the bus, behind the section reserved for whites. As more riders got

on, the bus filled up until there were no empty seats left. The aisle was jammed with passengers standing, mostly blacks and a few whites.

8   The driver stopped the bus and ordered black passengers seated behind the white section to get up and move further back, making more seats available for whites. Reluctantly, black riders gave up their seats and moved into the crowded aisle as whites took over the vacated seats.

9   Claudette didn't move. She knew she wasn't sitting in the **restricted** white section. She felt that she was far enough back to be **entitled** to her seat. A pregnant black woman was sitting next to her. When the driver insisted that the woman get up and stand in the aisle, a black man in the rear offered her his seat, then quickly left the bus to avoid trouble.

10 Claudette was now occupying a double seat alone. "Hey, get up!" the bus driver ordered. Still she refused to move. None of the white women standing would sit in the empty seat next to Claudette. It was against the law for blacks to sit in the same row as a white person.

11 The driver refused to move the bus. "This can't go on," he said. "I'm going to call the cops." He did, and when the police arrived, he demanded that Claudette be arrested.

12 "Aren't you going to get up?" one of the police officers asked.

13 "No," Claudette replied. "I don't have to get up. I paid my fare, so I don't have to get up." At school, Claudette had been studying the U.S. Constitution and the Bill of Rights, and she had taken those lessons to heart. "It's my constitutional right to sit here just as much as that [white] lady," she told the police. "It's my constitutional right!"

14 Blacks had been arrested before for talking back to white officials. Now it was Claudette's turn. She was crying and madder than ever when the police told her she was under arrest. "You have no right to do this," she protested. She struggled as they knocked her books aside, grabbed her wrists, and dragged her off the bus, and she screamed when they put on the handcuffs.

15 "I didn't know what was happening," she said later. "I was just angry. Like a teenager might be, I was just downright angry. It felt like I was helpless." She remained locked up at the city jail until she was bailed out later that day by the pastor of her church.

16 Under Montgomery's segregation laws, Claudette was in fact entitled to her seat behind the whites-only section. If no seats were available for blacks to move back to as additional white passengers boarded the bus, then they

NOTES

Skill:
Compare and
Contrast

I see similarities to
Freedom's Daughters.
The author mentions
the NAACP and
segregation. The author
of *Freedom Walkers*
describes how
Claudette stood up for
her rights and got
others to join her, much
like Barbara Johns did
when she gathered
student leaders for a
strike in *Freedom's
Daughters*.

were not required to give up their seats. That was the official **policy.** But in actual practice, whenever a white person needed a seat, the driver would order blacks to get up and move to the back of the bus, even when they had to stand in the aisle.

17 Prosecutors threw the book at Claudette. She was charged not only with violating the segregation laws, but also with assault and **battery** for resisting arrest. "She insisted she was colored and just as good as white," the surprised arresting officer told the judge at the court hearing.

18 Claudette's arrest galvanized the black community. E.D. Nixon, an influential black leader, came to the teenager's defense. Nixon was employed as a railroad sleeping car porter, but his passion was working to advance human rights. A rugged man with a forceful manner and commanding voice, he founded the Montgomery chapter of the National Association for the Advancement of Colored People (NAACP). Nixon was recognized by blacks and whites alike as a powerful presence in the black community, a vital force to be reckoned with. It was said that he knew every white policeman, judge, and government clerk in town, and he was always ready to help anyone in trouble.

19 When Nixon heard about Claudette Colvin's arrest, he got in touch with Clifford Durr, a liberal white attorney in Montgomery. Together they contacted Fred Gray, a twenty-four-year-old black lawyer who agreed to represent Colvin in court. Gray had grown up in Montgomery, attended Alabama State, and gone to Ohio for law school, because Alabama didn't have a law school for blacks. He was one of only two black attorneys in town.

20 After a brief trial in juvenile court, Claudette was found guilty of assault. She was fined and placed on probation in her parents' custody. She had expected to be cleared, and when the judge announced his verdict, she broke into agonized sobs that shook everyone in the crowded courtroom.

21 "The verdict was a bombshell!" Jo Ann Robinson recalled. "Blacks were as near a breaking point as they had ever been."

22 E.D. Nixon and other black leaders wanted to take the entire bus segregation issue into federal court. They hoped to demonstrate that segregated buses were illegal under the U.S. Constitution. But first they needed the strongest possible case-the arrest of a black rider who was above reproach, a person of unassailable character and reputation who could withstand the closest scrutiny. Claudette Colvin, Nixon felt, was too young and immature, too prone to emotional outbursts, to serve as standard-bearer for a long and expensive constitutional test case. As Nixon pointed out, she had fought with police, she came from the poorer side of black Montgomery, and it was later rumored

that she was pregnant. "I had to be sure I had somebody I could win with. . . to ask people to give us a half million dollars to fight discrimination on a bus line," Nixon said later.

23 In October 1955, several months after Claudette was convicted, Mary Louise Smith, an eighteen-year-old black girl, was arrested when she refused to move to the back of the bus so a white woman could take her seat. "[The driver] asked me to move three times," Smith recalled. "And I refused. I told him, 'I am not going to move out of my seat. I am not going to move anywhere. I got the privilege to sit here like anybody else does.'"

24 Smith's case did not create the furor that the Colvin case did, because Smith chose to plead guilty. She was fined five dollars. Once again, Nixon decided that Smith, like Colvin, wasn't the right person to inspire a battle against bus segregation.

25 Two months later, on December 1, 1955, another black woman boarded a city bus and found an empty seat just behind the white section. She was Rosa Parks.

✎ WRITE

PERSONAL RESPONSE: Referring to the story of Claudette Colvin, and to your own experience, write a speech about courage. Before you write, think about the following questions: What motivates courage? How is it driven by emotion? How is courage influenced by one's values and strong beliefs? How is it driven by conditions in our society?

Please note that excerpts and passages in the StudySync® library and this workbook are intended as touchstones to generate interest in an author's work. The excerpts and passages do not substitute for the reading of entire texts, and StudySync® strongly recommends that students seek out and purchase the whole literary or informational work in order to experience it as the author intended. Links to online resellers are available in our digital library. In addition, complete works may be ordered through an authorized reseller by filling out and returning to StudySync® the order form enclosed in this workbook.

Reading & Writing Companion

63

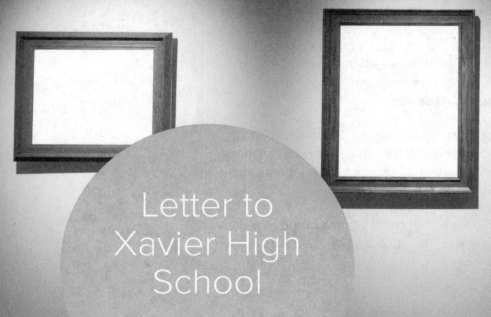

Letter to Xavier High School

INFORMATIONAL TEXT
Kurt Vonnegut
2013

Introduction

Kurt Vonnegut (1922–2007) is one of the most celebrated and influential American novelists of the postmodern era. His works include the classic novels Slaughterhouse-Five and Breakfast of Champions. In 2006, a group of students at Xavier High School wrote a letter to Vonnegut trying to convince him to visit their school. Though age prevented him from attending in person, his written response was quintessential Vonnegut. "[D]o art and do it for the rest of your lives," he wrote, even if it means singing in the shower, writing and then destroying a poem, or pretending to be Count Dracula. Create for the sake of creating. Vonnegut passed away less than six months later at the age of 84.

"... starting right now, do art and do it for the rest of your lives"

Copyright © BookheadEd Learning, LLC

NOTES

1   Dear Xavier High School, and Ms. Lockwood, and Messrs Perin, McFeely, Batten, Maurer and Congiusta:

2   I thank you for your friendly letters. You sure know how to cheer up a really old geezer (84) in his sunset years. I don't make public appearances any more because I now **resemble** nothing so much as an iguana.

3   What I had to say to you, moreover, would not take long, to wit: **Practice** any art, music, singing, dancing, acting, drawing, painting, sculpting, poetry, fiction, essays, reportage, no matter how well or badly, not to get money and fame, but to experience becoming, to find out what's inside you, to make your soul grow.

4   Seriously! I mean starting right now, do art and do it for the rest of your lives. Draw a funny or nice picture of Ms. Lockwood, and give it to her. Dance home after school, and sing in the shower and on and on. Make a face in your mashed potatoes. Pretend you're Count Dracula.

5   Here's an assignment for tonight, and I hope Ms. Lockwood will flunk you if you don't do it: Write a six line poem, about anything, but rhymed. No fair tennis without a net. Make it as good as you possibly can. But don't tell anybody what you're doing. Don't show it or **recite** it to anybody, not even your girlfriend or parents or whatever, or Ms. Lockwood. OK?

6   Tear it up into teeny-weeny pieces, and **discard** them into widely separated trash recepticals [sic]. You will find that you have already been gloriously rewarded for your poem. You have experienced becoming, learned a lot more about what's inside you, and you have made your soul grow.

7   God bless you all!

Kurt Vonnegut

WRITE

PERSONAL RESPONSE: Vonnegut claims that any creative pursuit, whether as a hobby or career, has a significant and positive impact on a person's life. In your opinion, do you think schools today do enough to nurture and promote creativity? Support your response with evidence from the text as well as your own experiences.

Freedom Daughters

The Unsung Heroines of the Civil Rights Movement from 1830 to 1970

INFORMATIONAL TEXT
Lynne Olson
2001

Introduction

Lynne Olson (b. 1949) is an American author and historian who includes the story of Barbara Johns in *Freedom's Daughters*, her book about the female champions of civil rights frequently neglected in history books. In 1950, Barbara Johns was a high school student in Farmville, Virginia who ran out of patience with the collection of tar-paper shacks they called a high school, and organized a student strike to take action.

"For six months, the students planned their strategy. They put it into effect on April 23, 1951."

From Chapter 4: Lighting the Fuse

1   Although she had spent much of her early life there, Farmville was a place where Barbara Johns never really felt she belonged. The seat of Prince Edward County, Farmville was a trading center for tobacco and lumber, a town that didn't seem to have changed much since Robert E. Lee and Ulysses S. Grant had separately stopped there in April 1865 on their way to end the Civil War at Appomattox Court House. In 1951, local blacks were barred from the hotel where the generals had rested, just as they were barred from Farmville's restaurants, its drugstore counters, and its only movie theater, bowling alley, and swimming pool. And, of course, its all-white public schools. The school Barbara Johns attended, Moton High School, featured "temporary" buildings that were really just tar-paper shacks, and classrooms that were usually too stuffy and hot in the fall and spring and too cold in the winter. For years, the all-white school district had been promising the black community a new school, but somehow it was never built. The blacks, despite their resentment, did not dare complain too loudly.

2   Barbara Johns could not understand such **docility**. Pretty and bright, she had always been an outspoken child; family members said she took after her uncle Vernon, the pastor of the Dexter Avenue Baptist Church in Montgomery, Alabama. The family didn't mean that as much of a compliment, but Barbara, who idolized her uncle, took it as one anyway. Vernon Johns was a hot-tempered crusader for civil rights, who railed at his congregation and other blacks for their **complacency** in the face of racial and other social injustice. Not much loved by the **affluent** black members of his church, he was destined to have a powerful influence on his young successor at Dexter Avenue, Martin Luther King, Jr.

3   When Johns visited Farmville, Barbara loved to hear him talk. "He was beyond the intellectual **scope** of everyone around the county," she said. "I remember that white men would . . . listen to him speak and shake their heads, not understanding his language." As much as she hero-worshipped her uncle,

however, she didn't shy away from disagreeing with him. "We'd always be on opposite sides in an argument. I'm afraid we were both very **antagonistic**."

4   At Moton High School, Barbara Johns participated in the drama club, the chorus, and the student council. Those activities made it possible for her to travel to other black high schools around the state. Many, she couldn't help noticing, were in better shape than Moton. What bothered Johns and her fellow students most about their school were the tar-paper shacks, with their leaky roofs and pathetic woodstoves. An occasional motorist, driving by the school, would stop to ask the students what the shacks were. One man, told they were part of the school, responded: "School? Looks like a poultry farm!"

5   In the fall of 1950, Johns decided to take action on her own. She brought five other student leaders together for a **clandestine** student meeting in the bleachers of the school's athletic field. Farmville's black adults, she said, had made no headway in getting a new school. "Then," recalled one of the other students at the meeting, "she said our parents ask us to follow them but in some instances—and I remember her saying this very vividly—a little child shall lead them. She said we could make a move that would broadcast Prince Edward County all over the world."

6   For six months, the students planned their strategy. They put it into effect on April 23, 1951. Late that morning, Moton's principal, Boyd Jones, received a phone call from one of the conspirators, advising him that two of his students were about to be arrested by police at the Greyhound bus station. Jones left school in a hurry, never suspecting that the summons was a **ploy** to get him safely away so that a note with Jones's forged signature could be sent to each classroom, announcing an immediate school assembly. After the teachers and the school's 450 students gathered in the auditorium, the curtains on the stage parted and revealed Barbara Johns, not Boyd Jones, standing at the podium. She declared that the meeting was for students only and asked the teachers to leave. When some teachers protested, Johns removed one of her shoes and smacked it on a bench, "I want you out of here!" she shouted. At that, all the teachers left, some with student escorts. Then Johns got down to business. The time had come, she said, for dramatic action. Joined by the other student organizers, she called for a student strike and produced hand-lettered picket signs proclaiming "We Want a New School or None at All" and "Down with the Tar-Paper Shacks." The students cheered and marched out of the auditorium, with Barbara Johns in the vanguard.

7   The strike leaders sent a letter to the NAACP in Richmond that same afternoon. "We hate to impose as we are doing," the letter began, "but under the circumstances we are facing, we have to ask for your help." Three days later, two top civil rights lawyers were on their way to Farmville. By this time, the

Skill:
Central or Main Idea

I can see that Barbara makes a decision to do something about the horrible conditions of her school, so she is a leader. I think the central idea of this text is that a young, African American girl stood up to injustice and was going to help get a better school.

Skill:
Central or Main Idea

I believe these details support the idea that Barbara is standing up for injustice as she attempts to accomplish her goal.

NOTES

Skill:
Central or Main
Idea

The author of
Freedom's Daughters
also mentions the
NAACP and
segregation, so these
terms must be
important to know
when reading about the
Civil Rights Movement.

NAACP had already decided to challenge "separate but equal" in favor of total desegregation. Although there may have been, as Richard Kluger has written, "no less promising place in all Virginia to wage the fight for equal schools," the NAACP lawyers were willing to try. In a shabby basement meeting room of a local church, they told the students and some parents that the NAACP would help them *only* if they were prepared to go for broke— desegregation or nothing—and then only if the students could demonstrate that they had the support of the adults in the black community. The strikers were stunned but enthusiastic. "It seemed like reaching for the moon," said Barbara Johns.

First Read

Read "Freedom's Daughters: The Unsung Heroines of the Civil Rights Movement from 1830 to 1970." After you read, complete the Think Questions below.

☁ THINK QUESTIONS

1. How was Barbara Johns similar to her uncle Vernon? What was their relationship like? Support your response with evidence from the text.

2. What can you infer about the people in the Farmville school district? Support your response with textual evidence.

3. Why did Barbara Johns decide to plan a student boycott? Cite evidence from the text in your response.

4. Use context to determine the meaning of the word **ploy** as it is used in *Freedom's Daughters*. Write your definition of *ploy* here and include an explanation of how details in the text helped your understanding.

5. Compare the meaning of **complacency** with words that are slightly different in meaning: *contentment, satisfaction, delight,* and *euphoria.* Check the different connotations in a dictionary.

Please note that excerpts and passages in the StudySync® library and this workbook are intended as touchstones to generate interest in an author's work. The excerpts and passages do not substitute for the reading of entire texts, and StudySync® strongly recommends that students seek out and purchase the whole literary or informational work in order to experience it as the author intended. Links to online resellers are available in our digital library. In addition, complete works may be ordered through an authorized reseller by filling out and returning to StudySync® the order form enclosed in this workbook.

Reading & Writing Companion   **71**

Skill:
Central or Main Idea

Use the Checklist to analyze Central or Main Idea in "Freedom's Daughters: The Unsung Heroines of the Civil Rights Movement from 1830 to 1970." Refer to the sample student annotations about Central or Main Idea in the text.

••• CHECKLIST FOR CENTRAL OR MAIN IDEA

In order to identify the central idea of a text, note the following:

- ✓ the topic or subject of the text
- ✓ the central or main idea, if it is explicitly stated
- ✓ the central or main idea, if it is explicitly stated
- ✓ details in the text that convey the theme

To determine the central idea of a text and how it is conveyed through particular details consider the following questions:

- ✓ What main idea do the details in one or more paragraphs explain or describe?
- ✓ What bigger idea do all the paragraphs support?
- ✓ What is the best way to state the central idea? How might you summarize the text and message?
- ✓ How do particular details in the text convey the central idea?

Skill:
Central or Main Idea

Reread paragraphs 2–3 of "Freedom's Daughters: The Unsung Heroines of the Civil Rights Movement from 1830 to 1970." Then, using the Checklist on the previous page, answer the multiple-choice questions below.

⟳ YOUR TURN

1. This question has two parts. First, answer Part A. Then, answer Part B

Part A: Which of the following best represents the central or main idea of the excerpt?

- ○ A. Barbara Johns was meant to stand up and fight injustice.
- ○ B. Martin Luther King, Jr. was a strong influencer.
- ○ C. Barbara Johns admired her uncle Vernon's speeches.
- ○ D. Montgomery, Alabama was central to the Civil Rights Movement.

Part B: Which of the following details best supports the central or main idea in Part A?

- ○ A. ". . . she had always been an outspoken child; family members said she took after her uncle Vernon . . ."
- ○ B. "The family didn't mean that as much of a compliment, but Barbara, who idolized her uncle, took it as one anyway."
- ○ C. "Not much loved by the affluent black members of his church, he was destined to have a powerful influence . . ."
- ○ D. "He was beyond the intellectual scope of everyone around the county . . .'"

Please note that excerpts and passages in the StudySync® library and this workbook are intended as touchstones to generate interest in an author's work. The excerpts and passages do not substitute for the reading of entire texts, and StudySync® strongly recommends that students seek out and purchase the whole literary or informational work in order to experience it as the author intended. Links to online resellers are available in our digital library. In addition, complete works may be ordered through an authorized reseller by filling out and returning to StudySync® the order form enclosed in this workbook.

Reading & Writing Companion   **73**

Skill:
Compare and Contrast

Use the Checklist to analyze Compare and Contrast in "Freedom's Daughters: The Unsung Heroines of the Civil Rights Movement from 1830 to 1970." Refer to the sample student annotations about Compare and Contrast in the text.

••• CHECKLIST FOR CENTRAL OR MAIN IDEA

In order to determine how to compare and contrast one author's presentation of events with that of another, use the following steps:

- ✓ first, choose two texts with similar subjects or topics, such as an autobiography and a biography of the same person, or a news report of an event and a narrative nonfiction account of the same event

- ✓ next, identify the author's approach to the subject in each genre

- ✓ after, explain how the point of view changes in each text

- ✓ finally, analyze ways in which the texts are similar and different in their presentation of specific events and information

  - whether the nonfiction narrative account contains dialogue that may not have been spoken, or may have been altered in some way

  - what the author of an autobiography might know that a biographer might never be able to uncover or research

To compare and contrast one author's presentation of events with that of another, consider the following questions:

- ✓ How does the author approach each topic or subject?

- ✓ What are the similarities and differences in the presentation of events in each text?

Skill:
Compare and Contrast

Reread paragraphs 5 and 6 of *Freedom Walkers: The Story of the Montgomery Bus Boycott* and paragraph 4 of "Freedom's Daughters: The Unsung Heroines of the Civil Rights Movement from 1830 to 1970." Then, using the Checklist on the previous page, answer the multiple-choice questions below.

⟳ YOUR TURN

1. Which of the following do both passages have in common?

   ○ A. They both present information about young men who were activists in the civil rights movement.

   ○ B. They both present information about women who came from families that were involved in the Civil Rights Movement

   ○ C. They both present information about women who came from families that were involved in the Civil Rights Movement.

   ○ D. They both highlight the unfair treatment of African Americans in regard to the poor condition of schools during the civil rights movement

Please note that excerpts and passages in the StudySync® library and this workbook are intended as touchstones to generate interest in an author's work. The excerpts and passages do not substitute for the reading of entire texts, and StudySync® strongly recommends that students seek out and purchase the whole literary or informational work in order to experience it as the author intended. Links to online resellers are available in our digital library. In addition, complete works may be ordered through an authorized reseller by filling out and returning to StudySync® the order form enclosed in this workbook.

Reading & Writing
Companion

75

Read the textual evidence from *Freedom Walkers* and *Freedom's Daughters* below. Then, using the Checklist on the previous page, complete the chart by choosing which piece of text evidence contrasts the author's presentation in each text.

⟳ YOUR TURN

	Text Evidence
A	"What bothered Johns and her fellow students most about their school were the tar-paper shacks, with their leaky roofs and pathetic woodstoves."
B	"During the next few years, other black riders were arrested and convicted for the same offense-sitting in seats reserved for whites."

Discrimination in *Freedom Walkers*	Discrimination in *Freedom's Daughters*

Close Read

Reread "Freedom's Daughters: The Unsung Heroines of the Civil Rights Movement from 1830 to 1970." As you reread, complete the Skills Focus questions below. Then use your answers and annotations from the questions to help you complete the Write activity.

◎ SKILLS FOCUS

1. Determine the main idea of "Freedom's Daughters: The Unsung Heroines of the Civil Rights Movement from 1830 to 1970" and identify the details that support it.

2. Find evidence in "Freedom's Daughters: The Unsung Heroines of the Civil Rights Movement from 1830 to 1970" and "Freedom Walkers: The Story of the Montgomery Bus Boycott," in order to compare and contrast how each author presents events of the civil rights movement.

3. Describe how Barbara Johns would answer the question, "What qualities of character matter most?" Use evidence from the text to support your response.

✏ WRITE

COMPARATIVE: In "Freedom Walkers: The Story of the Montgomery Bus Boycott," fifteen-year-old Claudette Colvin refuses to give up her seat on a bus. By staying seated, she stood up for the rights of all African Americans. In "Freedom's Daughters: The Unsung Heroines of the Civil Rights Movement from 1830 to 1970," another teenager, Barbara Johns, notices the unfair school conditions for African Americans and organizes a strike until the condition of her school is improved. Compare and contrast the main ideas of these two texts, noting how the authors present events in the civil rights movement. Be sure to use evidence from both texts in your response.

Please note that excerpts and passages in the StudySync® library and this workbook are intended as touchstones to generate interest in an author's work. The excerpts and passages do not substitute for the reading of entire texts, and StudySync® strongly recommends that students seek out and purchase the whole literary or informational work in order to experience it as the author intended. Links to online resellers are available in our digital library. In addition, complete works may be ordered through an authorized reseller by filling out and returning to StudySync® the order form enclosed in this workbook.

Reading & Writing Companion   **77**

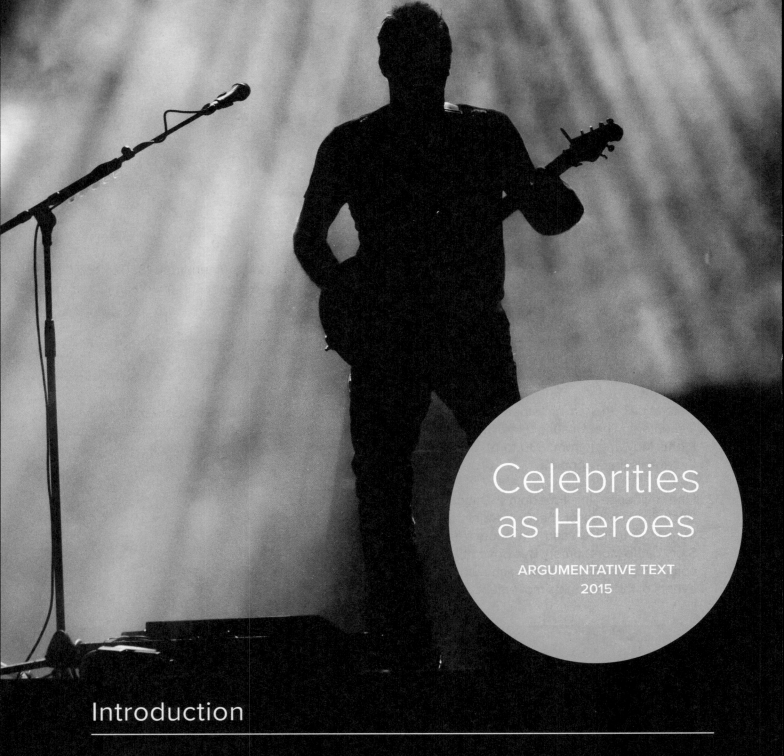

Celebrities as Heroes

ARGUMENTATIVE TEXT
2015

Introduction

There is no question that celebrities are frequently idolized as heroes, especially by young people. But do they deserve such admiration? The authors of these two articles have different opinions. One claims that most celebrities have not done enough to be called heroic, while the other argues that many celebrities do qualify as heroes for their achievements and cultural influence. Both writers present strong arguments and support their claims with evidence. Which do you think is more convincing?

"They may think that if they act like their idol, they too will become famous."

Celebrities as Heroes: What makes someone a hero?

Point: Celebrities Should Not Be Idolized as Heroes

NOTES

1   "Did you read what he said on Twitter? He's my hero!"

2   "Do you know what she did on vacation? She's my hero!"

3   "Did you hear how they finally tracked down the gang in the latest podcast? They're my heroes!"

4   "Did you see what she wore to that awards show? She's my hero!"

5   Today, many people use the word "hero" too lightly. They confuse the word "hero" with the word "celebrity." Right now, almost anyone can be a celebrity. But money, **notoriety**, and flamboyant behavior don't make someone a hero. Neither does playing the role of a hero on TV or in the movies. In fact, most celebrities don't deserve to be called heroes because they aren't heroes. They're people who are "celebrities" or "celebrated" for no other reason than because their fame has spread by word of mouth, the press, or social media. They may go to a thousand parties a month and are famous for being famous. We cannot regard these people as heroes in any way because they are all frivolous.

Skill:
Reasons and
Evidence

The writer has made the claim that celebrities should not be idolized as heroes. This is because most celebrities are not heroes. Then the writer adds to that reason by giving a definition of a celebrity as evidence.

7   What makes a hero? Heroes have been defined as people who have admirable qualities. These can include strength, honesty, courage, and perseverance. They have done something that helped others in some way. For example, by refusing to give up her seat on a bus, Rosa Parks became a hero for **civil** rights, and her action inspired others to fight for equality. Firefighters, police officers, soldiers, and regular citizens have often acted heroically, and they have saved people from attacks and natural disasters. Heroes can also be individuals who have made a difference in people's lives. These people might include teachers, parents, coaches, and mentors.

8   When celebrities are idolized just because they play heroes in movies and on television, they can end up overshadowing real heroes. They may get our attention, but they don't do much to change the world. This leaves young people with heroes who have little substance. The increase in this kind of hero worship is because more teenagers are using social media.

9   Psychologist Abby Aronowitz, Ph.D., says that the media is partly to blame for the hero worship of celebrities. She says that the media gives celebrities a lot of attention. However, many who work in the media claim that news about their idols is what people want to watch and read about. Celebrity sells.

9   Dr. Stuart Fischoff of the American Psychological Association says it's normal for people to idolize those who have fame and fortune. "We are sociologically preprogrammed to 'follow the leader,'" he says. However, if young people choose to idolize a celebrity who **indulges** in risky behavior, then they might be inspired to do the same. They may think that if they act like their idol, they too will become famous.

10   Many celebrities love that the media turns them into heroes, but some celebrities criticize these false images, and they don't want to be heroes. They don't want the pressure of being seen as role models. They don't want any mistakes they make to be reported. This will likely upset those who idolize them. However, young fans will continue to turn celebrities into heroes.

11   Convincing young people that celebrities do not make good role models or heroes will be difficult. So the media needs to focus on real heroes. Many can be found in history. Examples include Martin Luther King Jr., Eleanor Roosevelt, Gandhi, and Abraham Lincoln. There are also many everyday men and women who have acted heroically. Even though they have flaws as all humans do, their courage can inspire others. These people will still be heroes long after some celebrities are no longer remembered.

Skill:
Reasons and Evidence

The writer is trying to support his claim that celebrities are not heroes by saying that celebrities don't want to be labeled that way. However, the writer doesn't provide any evidence to back up this claim. This point would be stronger if he had a quote from a real celebrity.

NOTES

"If fans confuse mere celebrities with real heroes, they rob themselves of good role models."

Counterpoint: Celebrities Can Be Cultural Heroes

12   After the baseball game is over, young fans line up to get autographs from their favorite players. The player who hit the home run that won the game is greeted with cheers. One fan yells, "You're my hero!"

13   Many actors, singers, and television stars are also idolized. They are all famous celebrities, but are they also heroes? Do they deserve or even want such admiration?

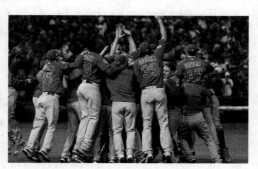

14   Society can be quick to sneer at celebrities who are idolized. Many people say that any contribution a celebrity makes is minor. Some people dismiss celebrities just because they *are* celebrities. Yet,

Celebrities might be considered heroes because of their outstanding achievements, like winning the World Series.

there are many celebrities who are true heroes. These individuals may have struggled courageously to reach their goals and made outstanding achievements in their fields—sports, movies, music, fashion—that can inspire others.

15   Striving to be the best one can be at a sport or profession is not easy. It can require extraordinary skill. It takes determination, self-sacrifice, and dedication. Celebrities who struggle and work to be the best in their field can set good examples as role models.

16   Dr. Eric Hollander at the Mt. Sinai School of Medicine in New York City says "Celebrities can have a positive **influence** on our lives, with positive messages." This is especially true when fans appreciate a celebrity's abilities and achievements. They may idolize a soccer player's genuine ability to play well and score points. This admiration may lead young fans to work harder when they play soccer. They want to be like their hero.

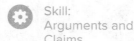 Skill: Arguments and Claims

The first and last sentences of paragraph 15 claim that celebrities who work hard should be admired, which supports the argument that celebrities can be heroes.

**Skill:
Arguments and
Claims**

*In paragraph 17, the
author lists two actors
and explains how they
have helped others. The
specific examples of
charitable celebrities
support the argument
that some celebrities
are heroic.*

17   In addition, some celebrities have made outstanding contributions to charitable causes. Paul Newman was called one of the best actors of his time, but he also founded a food company that donates all of its profits to charity. In 2010 actress Sandra Bullock gave money to several charitable organizations. This was to help survivors of the 2010 earthquake in Haiti. Celebrities like these have a positive effect on people. Helping others is definitely something that heroes do.

18   Still, it's up to the fans to choose their heroes carefully. Fans need to know what qualities real heroes have and to look for these qualities in celebrities. They need to ask themselves if they are worshiping celebrities just because these people are famous or because they are true heroes. If fans confuse mere celebrities with real heroes, they rob themselves of good role models.

19   It's also up to the media to pay more attention to celebrities who are true role models. This is not always easy. Some celebrities are not necessarily looking for the media to shine a spotlight on their actions. They are involved in helping refugees, fighting for **conservation**, or working on other issues important to them. They aren't doing these things to increase their fame or to be admired as heroes.

20   Do people need heroes? Do dogs bark? All people need someone they can look up to and admire. If we are clear about the qualities we admire, we will be able to find many true role models among people we think of as "celebrities." But the individuals we choose to call our "heroes" can't be just any celebrities. They should be people who, by example or action, are trying to make a difference in other people's lives. Still, if you really believe in freedom, you should support the rights of people to choose whatever heroes they want.

First Read

Read "Celebrities as Heroes." After you read, complete the Think Questions below.

 THINK QUESTIONS

1. What is the main claim in the Point article? Use specific evidence from the text to support your answer.

2. What is the main claim in the Counterpoint article? Use specific evidence from the text to support your answer.

3. Why might celebrities want or not want to be viewed as heroes? Use specific evidence from the text to support your answer.

4. Use context clues to determine the meaning of the word **indulges** as it is used in paragraph 9 of the Point essay. Write your definition of *indulges* here and explain how you figured it out.

5. Read the following dictionary entry:

civil

civ•il \siv(ə)l\ *adjective*

1. related to the people living in a country
2. polite or courteous
3. relating to public business or gatherings

Which definition most closely matches the meaning of **civil** as it is used in paragraph 6? Write the correct definition of *civil* here and explain how you figured out the proper meaning.

Please note that excerpts and passages in the StudySync® library and this workbook are intended as touchstones to generate interest in an author's work. The excerpts and passages do not substitute for the reading of entire texts, and StudySync® strongly recommends that students seek out and purchase the whole literary or informational work in order to experience it as the author intended. Links to online resellers are available in our digital library. In addition, complete works may be ordered through an authorized reseller by filling out and returning to StudySync® the order form enclosed in this workbook.

Reading & Writing Companion   **83**

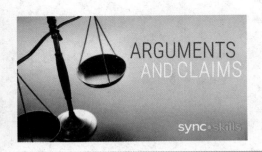

Skill:
Arguments and Claims

Use the Checklist to analyze Arguments and Claims in "Celebrities as Heroes ." Refer to the sample student annotations about Arguments and Claims in the text.

••• CHECKLIST FOR ARGUMENTS AND CLAIMS

In order to trace the argument and specific claims, do the following:

- ✓ identify clues that reveal the author's opinion in the title, introduction, or conclusion
- ✓ note the first and last sentence of each body paragraph for specific claims that help to build the author's argument
- ✓ list the information that the writer introduces in sequential order
- ✓ use a different color highlight to distinguish the writer's argument, claims, reasoning, and evidence
- ✓ describe the speaker's argument in your own wordsr

To evaluate the argument and specific claims, consider the following questions:

- ✓ Does the writer support each claim with reasoning and evidence?
- ✓ Am I able to distinguish claims that are supported by reasons and evidence from those that are not?
- ✓ Do the writer's claims work together to support the writer's overall argument?
- ✓ Which claims are not supported, if any?

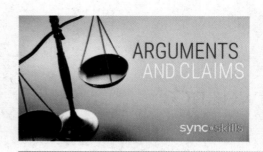

Skill:
Arguments and Claims

Reread paragraphs 8 and 9 of the Counterpoint argument. of "Celebrities as Heroes." Then, using the Checklist on the previous page, answer the multiple-choice questions below.

⟳ YOUR TURN

1. This question has two parts. First, answer Part A. Then, answer Part B.

Part A: What claim is the author making in paragraph 8?

- ○ A. We should pay attention to the celebrities who try to make the world a better place.
- ○ B. All celebrities are heroes.
- ○ C. Most celebrities do not work on important issues, but should be considered heroes.
- ○ D. We should pay attention to celebrities who do not work on important issues.

Part B: Which of the following sentences best supports the claim from Part A?

- ○ A. "Do people need heroes?"
- ○ B. "They should be people who, by example or action, are trying to make a difference in other people's lives."
- ○ C. "All people need someone they can look up to and admire."
- ○ D. "Still, if you really believe in freedom, you should support the rights of people to choose whatever heroes they want."

Please note that excerpts and passages in the StudySync® library and this workbook are intended as touchstones to generate interest in an author's work. The excerpts and passages do not substitute for the reading of entire texts, and StudySync® strongly recommends that students seek out and purchase the whole literary or informational work in order to experience it as the author intended. Links to online resellers are available in our digital library. In addition, complete works may be ordered through an authorized reseller by filling out and returning to StudySync® the order form enclosed in this workbook.

Reading & Writing Companion   85

Skill:
Reasons and Evidence

Use the Checklist to analyze Reasons and Evidence in "Celebrities as Heroes." Refer to the sample student annotations about Reasons and Evidence in the text.

••• CHECKLIST FOR REASONS AND EVIDENCE

In order to identify claims that are supported by reasons and evidence, do the following:

- ✓ look for the argument the author is making
- ✓ identify the claim or the main idea of the argument
- ✓ find the reasons and evidence that support the claim

To distinguish claims that are supported by reasons and evidence from claims that are not, consider the following questions:

- ✓ What reasons does the author give to support his claim?
- ✓ What kinds of evidence does the author include to support his or her reasons?
- ✓ Does each piece of evidence support the claim? Why or why not?
- ✓ Are there any claims that are not supported by reasons and evidence? If so, what kinds of reasons or evidence would the author need to include?

Skill:
Reasons and Evidence

Reread paragraphs 7–9 from the Point argument from "Celebrities as Heroes." Then, using the Checklist on the previous page, answer the multiple-choice questions below.

⟳ YOUR TURN

1. The kind of evidence used in paragraph 9 is —

   ○ A. a specific example
   ○ B. a quotation and expert opinion
   ○ C. numerical data
   ○ D. facts

2. How does the writer use the evidence in paragraph 9?

   ○ A. to support a claim that idolizing celebrities is not normal behavior
   ○ B. to warn that all celebrities indulge in risky behavior
   ○ C. to show how young people's normal behavior can turn into risky behavior
   ○ D. to emphasize that many young people need psychiatric help

3. Which of these three paragraphs supports the writer's argument the least?

   ○ A. paragraph 7
   ○ B. paragraph 8
   ○ C. paragraph 9
   ○ D. they all equally support the argument

Please note that excerpts and passages in the StudySync® library and this workbook are intended as touchstones to generate interest in an author's work. The excerpts and passages do not substitute for the reading of entire texts, and StudySync® strongly recommends that students seek out and purchase the whole literary or informational work in order to experience it as the author intended. Links to online resellers are available in our digital library. In addition, complete works may be ordered through an authorized reseller by filling out and returning to StudySync® the order form enclosed in this workbook.

Reading & Writing
Companion

87

Close Read

Reread "Celebrities as Heroes." As you reread, complete the Skills Focus questions below. Then use your answers and annotations from the questions to help you complete the Write activity.

◎ SKILLS FOCUS

1. Identify evidence that supports the Point claim that celebrities should not be idolized as heroes and the Counterpoint claim that celebrities can be cultural heroes. Explain how well the evidence or reasons support each claim.

2. Identify examples of claims that aren't supported by reasons or evidence in the Point and Counterpoint arguments. Explain what effect those unsupported claims have on the authors' arguments.

3. Highlight evidence from the Point or Counterpoint argument that suggests that character matters when determining whether a celebrity might qualify as a hero. Explain how the evidence supports the claim.

✏ WRITE

ARGUMENTATIVE: Which of the two arguments is less persuasive? In your response, include an analysis of the arguments, claims, reasons, and evidence the author uses in the argument you feel is less persuasive. Explain why you cannot commit to that argument by citing textual evidence from both texts to support your opinion.

Famous

POETRY
Naomi Shihab Nye
1995

Introduction

The word "famous" is used a dozen times over in Naomi Shihab Nye's relatively short poem of the same title. Yet the words "star," "celebrity," and even "fans" are not found anywhere in Nye's nine stanzas. Instead, Nye creates a new definition of her titular word based on relationships that exist in nature and everyday life. Nye is an American poet and the daughter of a Palestinian refugee, born in St. Louis and raised in San Antonio and Jerusalem. She is known for exploring the mundane and overlooked elements around us, both on full display in "Famous."

"The tear is famous, briefly, to the cheek."

Skill:
Poetic Elements and Structure

Nye uses the same pattern in these stanzas. First, she names an item. Then, she tells to whom or what the item is famous. This repetition creates a pattern that in turn, creates the structure of the poem.

Skill:
Poetic Elements and Structure

The structure of the poem changes at line 15. Instead of naming an item and saying to what or whom it is famous, Nye starts the last two stanzas with the phrase "I want to be famous."

1 The river is famous to the fish.

2 The loud voice is famous to silence,
3 which knew it would **inherit** the earth
4 before anybody said so.

5 The cat sleeping on the fence is famous to the birds
6 watching him from the birdhouse.

7 The tear is famous, **briefly**, to the cheek.

8 The idea you carry close to your **bosom**
9 is famous to your bosom.

10 The boot is famous to the earth,
11 more famous than the dress shoe,
12 which is famous only to floors.

13 The bent photograph is famous to the one who carries it
14 and not at all famous to the one who is pictured.

15 I want to be famous to shuffling men
16 who smile while crossing streets,
17 sticky children in grocery lines,
18 famous as the one who smiled back.

19 I want to be famous in the way a pulley is famous,
20 or a buttonhole, not because it did anything **spectacular,**
21 but because it never forgot what it could do.

"Famous" from *Words Under the Words: Selected Poems* by Naomi Shihab Nye, copyright © 1995. Reprinted with the permission of Far Corner Books.

Copyright © BookheadEd Learning, LLC

First Read

Read "Famous." After you read, complete the Think Questions below.

THINK QUESTIONS

1. By the standards of the speaker, what does it mean to be famous? Cite two of the examples the speaker calls "famous" and explain why they are.

2. Why is the boot more famous than the dress shoe? Explain the meaning behind this description.

3. What makes the speaker want to be famous "the way a pulley is famous, / or a buttonhole" in the final stanza of the poem? What is significant about these objects?

4. Find the word **inherit** in stanza 2 of "Famous." Use context clues in the surrounding lines, as well as the line in which the word appears, to determine the word's meaning. Write your definition here and identify clues that helped you to figure out the meaning.

5. Which context clues helped you determine the meaning of **spectacular** in the last stanza? Use these to write your own definition of the word, and then check a dictionary to confirm.

Skill:
Poetic Elements and Structure

Use the Checklist to analyze Poetic Elements and Structure in "Famous." Refer to the sample student annotations about Poetic Elements and Structure in the text.

••• CHECKLIST FOR POETIC ELEMENTS AND STRUCTURE

In order to identify elements of poetic structure, note the following:

- ✓ how the words and lines are arranged

- ✓ the form and overall structure of the poem

- ✓ the rhyme, rhythm, and meter, if present

- ✓ how the arrangement of lines and stanzas in the poem contribute to the poem's theme, or message

To analyze how a particular stanza fits into the overall structure of a text and contributes to the development of the theme, consider the following questions:

- ✓ What poetic form does the poet use? What is the structure?

- ✓ How do the lengths of the lines and stanzas affect the meaning?

- ✓ How does a poem's stanza fit into the structure of the poem overall?

- ✓ How does the form and structure affect the poem's meaning?

- ✓ In what way does a specific stanza contribute to the poem's theme?

Skill:
Poetic Elements and Structure

Reread lines 15–21 from "Famous." Then, using the Checklist on the previous page, answer the multiple-choice questions below.

YOUR TURN

1. How does the change in point of view in lines 15 and 19 affect the meaning of the poem?

   ○ A. The speaker shows that not everyone can be famous.
   ○ B. The speaker shows value for traditional fame.
   ○ C. The speaker shows that everyone can be important to someone.
   ○ D. The speaker shows the unimportance of fame.

2. Which line from the poem best describes the theme?

   ○ A. Line 15: I want to be famous to shuffling men
   ○ B. Line 17: Sticky children in grocery lines
   ○ C. Line 18: Famous as the one who smiled back
   ○ D. Line 21: But because it never forgot what it could do

Please note that excerpts and passages in the StudySync® library and this workbook are intended as touchstones to generate interest in an author's work. The excerpts and passages do not substitute for the reading of entire texts, and StudySync® strongly recommends that students seek out and purchase the whole literary or informational work in order to experience it as the author intended. Links to online resellers are available in our digital library. In addition, complete works may be ordered through an authorized reseller by filling out and returning to StudySync® the order form enclosed in this workbook.

Reading & Writing
Companion

93

Close Read

Reread "Famous." As you reread, complete the Skills Focus questions below. Then use your answers and annotations from the questions to help you complete the Write activity.

◎ SKILLS FOCUS

1. Examine Nye's open-form poem. Explain how this structure and other poetic elements contribute to the poem's theme.

2. A poem's theme is the message the poet is trying to deliver. Identify how the poet's use of comparing and contrasting helps you infer a theme in "Famous." Explain the theme using specific lines or stanzas from the poem.

3. Think about the message Nye is delivering about the true nature of fame. Highlight evidence in the poem that reveals the qualities of character that represent true fame. Explain what these qualities are.

✏ WRITE

LITERARY ANALYSIS: In her poem, Naomi Shihab Nye shakes up most people's ideas about what it means to be famous. Fame isn't about celebrity; it's about what's important. How does Nye's use of poetic elements and structure contribute to this theme? Be sure to cite evidence from the poem in your response.

Argumentative Writing Process: Plan

PLAN	DRAFT	REVISE	EDIT AND PUBLISH

Reading true stories about influential people, such as Malala Yousafzai, can help us identify characteristics and actions that we consider noble or just. Reading about fictional characters who must face familiar and realistic struggles, like Margot in "All Summer in a Day," can help us develop empathy, or understanding. The texts in this unit feature a mix of the two—individuals demonstrating their personal best and authors and poets who share their ideas on the qualities of character that matter most.

WRITING PROMPT

As part of a school-wide character-building initiative, your school will be hosting a book club. The purpose of this club is to give all students an opportunity to read and discuss two texts (one informational and one literary) that help teach the qualities of character that matter most. To choose the texts you will read, your school has decided to let students submit proposals.

After reading the texts from the *Personal Best* unit, write a proposal in which you argue which texts would be the most effective for a school-wide book club. In your proposal, choose one informational and one literary text. Use textual evidence to help support an argument and explain how both of the texts you have chosen develop a theme or a main idea that communicates the qualities of character that matter most. Make sure your proposal includes the following:

- an introduction
- a thesis statement
- coherent body paragraphs with claims
- reasons and relevant evidence

- transitions
- a formal style
- a conclusion

Writing to Sources

As you gather ideas and information from the texts in the unit, be sure to:

- include a claim
- address counterclaims

- use evidence from multiple sources
- avoid overly relying on one source

Introduction to Argumentative Writing

An argumentative essay is a form of persuasive writing where the writer makes a claim about a topic and then provides evidence—facts, details, examples, and quotations—to convince readers to accept and agree with the writer's claim. In order to provide convincing supporting evidence for an argumentative essay, the writer must often do outside research as well as cite the sources of the evidence that are presented in the essay.

A **literary analysis** is a form of argumentative writing that tries to persuade readers to accept the writer's interpretation of a literary text. Good literary analysis writing builds an argument with a strong claim, convincing reasons, relevant textual evidence, and a clear structure with an introduction, body paragraphs, and a conclusion. The characteristics of argumentative and literary analysis writing include:

- an introduction
- a claim or thesis
- textual evidence

- transitions
- a formal style
- a conclusion

As you continue with this Extended Writing Project, you'll receive more instruction and practice at crafting each of the characteristics of argumentative writing to create your own literary analysis.

Please note that excerpts and passages in the StudySync® library and this workbook are intended as touchstones to generate interest in an author's work. The excerpts and passages do not substitute for the reading of entire texts, and StudySync® strongly recommends that students seek out and purchase the whole literary or informational work in order to experience it as the author intended. Links to online resellers are available in our digital library. In addition, complete works may be ordered through an authorized reseller by filling out and returning to StudySync® the order form enclosed in this workbook.

Reading & Writing Companion   **97**

Before you get started on your own literary analysis text, read this argument that one student, Samrah, wrote in response to the writing prompt. As you read the Model, highlight and annotate the features of argumentative writing that Samrah included in her literary analysis.

 NOTES

☰ STUDENT MODEL

1   One quality of character that matters is bravery. Sometimes bravery means standing up for an idea or taking on bullies. That's what Malala Yousafzai did. The Taliban said she couldn't go to school. She went anyway and got shot. Now she speaks out for the right of all kids to go to school. For example, Malala says, "Education is education. We should learn everything and then choose which path to follow. Education is neither Eastern nor Western. It is human." Similarly, Priscilla, in "Priscilla and the Wimps," also stands up to bullies. Only these bullies are actually at her school. She's a loner but she takes action and speaks up when her friend gets bullied. Both Malala and Priscilla bravely stand up for what's right. Therefore, I nominate "Malala Yousafzai—Nobel Lecture" and the short story "Priscilla and the Wimps."

2   First, students will relate to the gripping story Malala tells about standing up to the Taliban. Malala is a young person with "a thirst for education" that the Taliban tried to end. When they said she and her classmates couldn't go to school anymore, Malala had two options. She could "remain silent and wait to be killed" or she could "speak up and then be killed." The Taliban shot her on her school bus, but she says "neither their ideas nor the bullets could win." Students will be inspired by her courage and strong beliefs.

3   "Priscilla and the Wimps" is an entertaining short story about a girl named Priscilla who stands up to a gang called "Klutter's Kobras." The gang, led by Monk Klutter, forces kids to pay up so they don't get "barred from the cafeteria" or worse. Most of the boys have "blue bruises" from getting beaten up. When one of the Kobras attacks Priscilla's only friend, Melvin, she steps in. Priscilla is quiet, large, and strong. With one "chop," she "breaks the Kobra's hold on Melvin's throat." She calls the Kobra a "wimp" and says she doesn't even know who Monk Klutter is. When Monk tries to grab Melvin, Priscilla puts him in a hammerlock. Students will laugh out loud reading this story while witnessing bravery in action.

4   Both of these texts tell a story that will affect readers. However, what is most important is how each text teaches a message: You don't have to be an adult or big and powerful to be brave. We kids complain a lot about school; however, Malala's speech might make us see things differently. Malala recovered. She won the Nobel Peace Prize. Now she travels around the world fighting for the right of children to go to school. She tells the stories of children who live in Nigeria, India, and Syria. These are places where war or certain beliefs keep kids, especially girls, from going to school. Her speech is worth reading because it's a reminder that an education is a right not every kid in the world enjoys. Its message might make us feel more grateful for our school.

5   Priscilla, from "Priscilla and the Wimps," is also young and brave. In the text it states she "hardly says anything to anybody," but she takes action and speaks up when her friend gets bullied. Sometimes standing up to other kids can be intimidating. The narrator of the story, one of the scared kids, calls Priscilla's actions "a move of pure poetry." Priscilla inspires the narrator because she isn't afraid to take on the bad guys. Priscilla will certainly have that effect on readers, too. Any kid who's ever been bullied or just felt like an underdog will find this story interesting and satisfying to read.

6   These texts are the best fit for our book club because they show different ways of being brave. Malala faced threats and was nearly killed for wanting to go to school. She survived and now speaks to the world. In the text it states that when she speaks, it's in "the voice of those 66 million girls" that can't go to school. She is determined and brave. Priscilla is different. She's a loner who "was sort of above everything," but when her one friend is threatened, she takes on the school bully. Her act of bravery helps out the other kids. We should read these texts in our book club because they show how you have to be brave to stand up for what's right. If you want to get an education, you might have to fight for it. If you want freedom from bullies, sometimes you have to get tough. These are lessons in bravery that we can all benefit from.

WRITE

Writers often take notes about their ideas before they sit down to write. Think about what you've learned so far about organizing literary analysis writing to help you begin prewriting.

- Which two texts will you choose to write about in your proposal?

- What about each of these texts suggests the qualities of character that matter most?

- What textual evidence will you include to make your proposal convincing?

- What kind of text structure would best suit your purpose for writing?

Response Instructions

Use the questions in the bulleted list to write a one-paragraph summary. Your summary should describe what you will include in your essay.

Don't worry about including all of the details now; focus only on the most essential and important elements. You will refer back to this short summary as you continue through the steps of the writing process.

Skill:
Thesis Statement

••• CHECKLIST FOR THESIS STATEMENT

Before you begin writing your thesis statement, ask yourself the following questions:

- What is the prompt asking me to write about?

- What is the topic of my essay?

- What claim do I want to make about the topic of this essay? Is my opinion clear to my reader?

- Does my thesis statement introduce the body of my essay?

- Where should I place my thesis statement?

Here are some methods to introduce and develop your claim and topic:

- think about the topic and central idea of your essay

  > the central idea of an argument is stated as a claim, or what will be proven or shown to be true

  > identify as many claims as you intend to prove

- write a clear statement about the central idea or claim. Your thesis statement should:

  > let the reader anticipate the body of your essay

  > respond completely to the writing prompt

- consider the best placement for your thesis statement

  > if your response is short, you may want to get right to the point. Your thesis statement may be presented in the first sentence of the essay.

  > if your response is longer (as in a formal essay), you can build up your thesis statement. In this case, you can place your thesis statement at the end of your introductory paragraph.

Please note that excerpts and passages in the StudySync® library and this workbook are intended as touchstones to generate interest in an author's work. The excerpts and passages do not substitute for the reading of entire texts, and StudySync® strongly recommends that students seek out and purchase the whole literary or informational work in order to experience it as the author intended. Links to online resellers are available in our digital library. In addition, complete works may be ordered through an authorized reseller by filling out and returning to StudySync® the order form enclosed in this workbook.

Reading & Writing
Companion

101

YOUR TURN

Read the sentences below from a paragraph of Samrah's draft. Choose the sentence that best states the main idea of the paragraph.

Sentences
Her speech is worth reading because it reminds us that an education is a right that not every kid in the world enjoys.
We kids complain a lot about school; however, Malala's speech might make us see things differently.
However, what is most important is how each text teaches a message that you don't have to be a grown-up or big and powerful to be brave.
It might make us feel more grateful for our school.

 WRITE

Use the questions in the checklist to write a thesis statement for your proposal.

Skill: Organizing Argumentative Writing

As you consider how to organize your writing for your argumentative essay, use the following questions as a guide:

• What is my position on this topic?

• Have I chosen the best organizing structure to present my information?

• Can my claim be supported by logical reasoning and relevant evidence?

• Do I have enough evidence to support my claim?

Follow these steps to plan out the organization of your argumentative essay, including organizing your reasons and evidence clearly:

• identify your claim

> write a statement that will present your claim in the first paragraph

• choose an organizing structure that will present your claim effectively

• identify reasons and evidence that support your claim

• note that textual evidence can be proven to be true in other sources, and may be in the form of:

> numbers or statistics

> quotes from experts

> names or dates

> reference sources

Please note that excerpts and passages in the StudySync® library and this workbook are intended as touchstones to generate interest in an author's work. The excerpts and passages do not substitute for the reading of entire texts, and StudySync® strongly recommends that students seek out and purchase the whole literary or informational work in order to experience it as the author intended. Links to online resellers are available in our digital library. In addition, complete works may be ordered through an authorized reseller by filling out and returning to StudySync® the order form enclosed in this workbook.

Reading & Writing Companion   103

YOUR TURN

Read each claim and the descriptions of each writer's overall purpose for writing below. Then, complete the chart by writing the organizational text structure that would best develop the thesis and achieve the writer's overall purpose.

Organizational Text Structure Options			
listing advantages and disadvantages	problem and solution	cause and effect	compare and contrast

Claim	Purpose	Organizational Text Structure
To deal with the problem of vandalism in schools, surveillance cameras should be placed in several locations.	to show how the problem of vandalism can be solved	
Although many people prefer dogs, cats are really the best pet a person can have.	to show the differences and similarities between cat ownership and dog ownership	
To combat the issue of bullying, the administration has proposed a zero-tolerance policy, but there are some disadvantages with this policy.	to explain why a zero-tolerance-for-bullying policy might not be the best solution	
If the mayor agrees to allow the factory to be built beside the river, the effects on the environment could be terrible.	to explain what will happen if a factory is built next to a river	

✏ WRITE

Use the steps in the checklist to plan out the organization of your argumentative essay/literary analysis.

Skill: Reasons and Relevant Evidence

> ••• CHECKLIST FOR REASONS AND RELEVANT EVIDENCE

As you begin to determine what reasons and relevant evidence will support your claim(s), use the following questions as a guide:

- What is the claim (or claims) that I am making in my argument?
- Are the reasons I have included clear and easy to understand?
- What relevant evidence am I using to support this claim?
- Have I selected evidence from credible sources, and are they relevant to my claim?
- Am I quoting the source evidence accurately?

Use the following steps as a guide to help you determine how you will support your claim(s) with clear reasons and relevant evidence, using credible sources:

- identify the claim(s) you will make in your argument
- establish clear reasons for making your claim(s)
- select evidence from credible sources that will convince others to accept your claim(s)
  - > look for reliable and relevant sources of information online, such as government or educational websites
  - > search print resources such as books written by an expert or authority on a topic
- explain the connection between your claim(s) and the evidence selected

↻ YOUR TURN

Choose the best answer to each question.

1. The following is a section of text from a previous draft of Samrah's proposal. Samrah would like to add a sentence to support the idea that she has presented in the underlined sentence. Which of these could BEST follow and support the underlined sentence?

> In "Priscilla and the Wimps," Priscilla stands up to the bully Monk Klutter and his gang, the "Kobras." All the kids at the school are terrified of the gang because the Kobras collect money from them. <u>The kids pay up so they don't get "barred from the cafeteria" or worse.</u>

- ○ A. Priscilla is not afraid of Monk or the Kobras.
- ○ B. Most of the boys have "blue bruises" from getting beaten up.
- ○ C. Priscilla's friend Melvin is definitely afraid of the Kobras.
- ○ D. Any kid who has been bullied understands why.

2. The following is a paragraph from a previous draft of Samrah's proposal. Samrah has included a sentence that is not relevant to her literary analysis. Which sentence should be deleted from this paragraph?

> (1) When one of the Kobras attacks Melvin, Priscilla's only friend, she steps in. (2) Priscilla has difficulty making friends. (3) Large and strong, she "breaks the Kobra's hold on Melvin's throat" with one "chop." (4) She calls the Kobra a "wimp" and claims not to know who Monk Klutter is. (5) Priscilla puts Monk in a hammerlock when he tries to grab Melvin. (6) The narrator calls it "a move of pure poetry." (7) Then she stuffs Monk in a locker and walks away. (8) Priscilla isn't afraid to take on the bad guys.

- ○ A. sentence 2
- ○ B. sentence 3
- ○ C. sentence 5
- ○ D. sentence 8

✎ WRITE

Use the questions in the checklist to revise your proposal.

Argumentative Writing
Process: Draft

PLAN	DRAFT	REVISE	EDIT AND PUBLISH

You have already made progress toward writing your proposal. Now it is time to draft your proposal.

✎ WRITE

Use your plan and other responses in your Binder to draft your proposal. You may also have new ideas as you begin drafting. Feel free to explore those new ideas as you have them. You can also ask yourself these questions:

- Have I organized my ideas in a way that makes my argument clear to readers and responsive to the prompt?

- Is my thesis statement clearly stated, responsive to the prompt, and correctly placed?

- Have I supported my position with convincing reasons, evidence, and examples?

Before you submit your draft, read it over carefully. You want to be sure that you've responded to all aspects of the prompt.

Here is Samrah's draft of her proposal. As you read, identify details that Samrah includes in support of her thesis. As she continues to revise and edit her proposal, she will find and improve weak spots in her writing, as well as correct any language or punctuation mistakes.

NOTES

STUDENT MODEL: FIRST DRAFT

~~One quality of character that matters is bravery. Sometimes bravery means standing up for an idea or taking on bullies. That's what Malala Yousafzai did. The Taliban said her couldn't go to school. She went anyway and got shot. Now she speaks out for the right of all kids to go to school. Priscilla in "Priscilla and the Wimps" stands up to the bullies at her school. She's a loner, but she takes action and speaks up when they friend gets bullied. Both Malala and Priscilla bravely stand up for what's right. That's why I nominate "Malala Yousafzai's Nobel Lecture" and the short story "Priscilla and the Wimps."~~

Skill:
Introductions

Samrah reads her introduction. She wants to add a hook to grab the reader's attention. Therefore, Samrah adds a quote from Malala to clearly inform the reader of Malala's goal, and it provides an interesting hook for the reader.

One quality of character that matters is bravery. Sometimes bravery means standing up for an idea or taking on bullies. That's what Malala Yousafzai did. The Taliban said she couldn't go to school. She went anyway and got shot. Now she speaks out for the right of all kids to go to school. For example, Malala says, "Education is education. We should learn everything and then choose which path to follow. Education is neither Eastern nor Western. It is human." Similarly, Priscilla, in "Priscilla and the Wimps," also stands up to bullies. Only these bullies are actually at her school. She's a loner but she takes action and speaks up when her friend gets bullied. Both Malala and Priscilla bravely stand up for what's right. Therefore, I nominate "Malala Yousafzai—Nobel Lecture" and the short story "Priscilla and the Wimps."

~~In her speach Malala shows that you don't have to be a grown up or big and powerful to be brave. She is still a young person. But she "had a thirst for education" that the Taliban tried to end. The Taliban shot her on her school bus, but Malala recovered. She won the Nobel Peace Prize. Now she travels around the world fighting for the write of children to go to school in her country of Pakistan and all around the world. We kids complain a lot about school but Malala's speech might make we see things differently. It's message might make us feel more grateful for our school.~~

First, students will relate to the gripping story Malala tells about standing up to the Taliban. Malala is a young person with "a thirst for education" that the Taliban tried to end. When they said she and her classmates couldn't go to school anymore, Malala had two options. She could "remain silent and wait to be killed" or she could "speak up and then be killed." The Taliban shot her on her school bus, but she says "neither their ideas nor the bullets could win." Students will be inspired by her courage and strong beliefs.

"Priscilla and the Wimps" is a entertaining short story, written by Richard Peck, about a girl, Priscilla, who stands up to a gang called "Klutter's Kobras." The Kobras are led by Monk Klutter, who terrifies the kids at school by collecting money from them. They're afraid of Monk and his gang. They pay up so they don't get "barred from the cafeteria" or worse. Most of the boys have "blue bruises" from getting beaten up. Priscilla is quiet, large, and strong. When one of the Kobras attacks Priscilla's only friend Melvin she steps in. With one "chop," she "breaks the Kobra's hold on Melvin's throat." She calls the Kobra a "wimp." She says she doesn't know who Monk Klutter is. When Monk tries to grab Melvin Priscilla puts he in a hammer lock. The narrator one of the scared kids calls it "a move of pure poetry." Then she stuffs Monk in a locker and walks away. Priscilla isn't afraid to take on the bad guys. Its like it doesn't effect her. Any kid who's ever been bullied or just felt left out will find this story interesting and satisfying to read.

Both of these texts tell a story that will affect readers. However, what is most important is how each text teaches a message: You don't have to be an adult or big and powerful to be brave. We kids complain a lot about school; however, Malala's speech might make us see things differently. Malala recovered. She won the Nobel Peace Prize. Now she travels around the world fighting for the right of children to go to school. She tells the stories of children who live in Nigeria, India, and Syria. These are places where war or certain beliefs keep kids, especially girls, from going to school. Her speech is worth reading because it's a reminder that an education is a right not every kid in the world enjoys. Its message might make us feel more grateful for our school.

NOTES

Skill:
Style

Samrah wants to use domain-specific language in her writing. She decides to be specific and mention the Taliban by name. She also includes the phrase "and strong beliefs" in the last sentence because this language strongly relates to Malala's passion for education.

Skill:
Transitions

Samrah wants to use transitions to connect her ideas about what Malala went through, the message she is spreading, and why she is a great example for the quality of bravery. Samrah adds a paragraph to highlight these ideas and decides to use the word however *in two places to create cohesion among her ideas.*

NOTES

Skill:
Conclusions

Samrah decides to add "because they show different ways of being brave" to her first sentence in order to restate the thesis more clearly. She also adds quotes about Malala and Priscilla to include details that show the depth of her knowledge about bravery. Finally, Samrah concludes her paragraph with a strong statement relating to the quality of character at the center of her analysis: bravery.

~~These texts are the best fit for we book club. Malala faced threats and was nearly killed for wanting to go to school. She survived and now speaks to the world. She is determined and brave. Priscilla is different. When her one friend is threatened, she takes on the school bully. She act of bravery helps out the other kids. We should read these texts in our book club because they show how you have to be brave to stand up for what's right.~~

These texts are the best fit for our book club because they show different ways of being brave. Malala faced threats and was nearly killed for wanting to go to school. She survived and now speaks to the world. In the text it states that when she speaks, it's in "the voice of those 66 million girls" that can't go to school. She is determined and brave. Priscilla is different. She's a loner who "was sort of above everything," but when her one friend is threatened, she takes on the school bully. Her act of bravery helps out the other kids. We should read these texts in our book club because they show how you have to be brave to stand up for what's right. If you want to get an education, you might have to fight for it. If you want freedom from bullies, sometimes you have to get tough. These are lessons in bravery that we can all benefit from.

Skill:
Introductions

Before you write your introduction, ask yourself the following questions:

- What is my claim? How can I introduce my claim(s) so it is clear to readers?

- What is the best way to organize my ideas, concepts, reasons, and evidence in a clear and logical order?

- How will you "hook" your reader's interest? You might:

  > start with an attention-grabbing statement

  > begin with an intriguing question

  > use descriptive words to set a scene

Below are two strategies to help you introduce your topic and claim, and organize reasons and evidence clearly in an introduction:

- Peer Discussion

  > talk about your topic with a partner, explaining what you already know and your ideas about your topic

  > write notes about the ideas you have discussed and any new questions you may have

  > review your notes and think about what will be your claim or controlling idea

  > briefly state your claim or thesis

  > organize your reasons and evidence in an order that is clear to readers, presenting your reasons first followed by evidence

  > write a possible "hook"

Before you write your introduction, ask yourself the following questions:

- What is my claim? How can I introduce my claim(s) so it is clear to readers?
- What is the best way to organize my ideas, concepts, reasons, and evidence in a clear and logical order?
- How will you "hook" your reader's interest? You might:
    > start with an attention-grabbing statement
    > begin with an intriguing question
    > use descriptive words to set a scene

YOUR TURN

Choose the best answer to each question.

1. The following introduction is from an earlier draft of Samrah's essay. Which sentence should Samrah add at the beginning to hook her reader?

> Malala Yousafzai was brave. The Taliban said her couldn't go to school. She went anyway and got shot. Now she speaks out for the right of all kids to go to school. Priscilla in "Priscilla and the Wimps" stands up to the bullies at her school. She's a loner, but she takes action and speaks up when they friend gets bullied. Both Malala and Priscilla bravely stand up for what's right. Therefore, I nominate "Malala Yousafzai—Nobel Lecture" and the short story "Priscilla and the Wimps."

- ○ A. Have you ever been brave?
- ○ B. Bravery, the most important quality of character, can be shown by standing up to all types of bullies.
- ○ C. Priscilla was brave, but Malala was even braver.
- ○ D. Bravery is shown in many ways.

2. Samrah would like to add transitions in order to organize the ideas of her introduction more clearly. Which transition or transitional phrase could be added to the beginning of sentence 5?

> (1) Malala Yousafzai was brave. (2) The Taliban said her couldn't go to school. (3) She went anyway and got shot. (4) Now she speaks out for the right of all kids to go to school. (5) Priscilla in "Priscilla and the Wimps" stands up to the bullies at her school.

- ○ A. Likewise,
- ○ B. Then,
- ○ C. Finally,
- ○ D. However,

 WRITE

Use the questions in the checklist to revise the introduction of your literary analysis.

Skill:
Transitions

Before you revise your current draft to include transitions, think about:

- the key ideas you discuss in your body paragraphs
- the organizational structure of your essay
- the relationships among claim(s) and reasons

Next, reread your current draft and note areas in your essay where:

- the relationships between your claim(s) and the reasons and evidence are unclear, identifying places where you could add linking words or other transitional devices to make your argument more cohesive. Look for:

  > sudden jumps in your ideas

  > breaks between paragraphs where the ideas in the next paragraph are not logically following from the previous

Revise your draft to use words, phrases, and clauses to clarify the relationships among claim(s) and reasons, using the following questions as a guide:

- Are there unifying relationships between the claims, reasons, and evidence I present in my argument?
- Have I clarified, or made clear, these relationships?
- What linking words (such as conjunctions), phrases, or clauses could I add to my argument to clarify the relationships between the claims, reasons, and evidence I present?

YOUR TURN

Write each transition into the category of writing in which it would be most effective.

Transition Options	
A	meanwhile
B	for example
C	on the other hand

Type of Writing	Transition
informative	
narrative	
argumentative	

 YOUR TURN

Complete the chart by adding transitions into your literary analysis.

Transition	Transitional Sentence
although	
on the other hand	
however	
for example	

Skill:
Style

••• CHECKLIST FOR STYLE

First, reread the draft of your argumentative essay and identify the following:

- places where you use slang, contractions, abbreviations, and a conversational tone
- areas where you could use subject-specific or academic language in order to help persuade or inform your readers
- moments where you use first-person (*I*) or second person (*you*)
- areas where sentence structure lacks variety
- incorrect uses of the conventions of standard English for grammar, spelling, capitalization, and punctuation

Establish and maintain a formal style in your essay, using the following questions as a guide:

- Have I avoided slang in favor of academic language?
- Did I consistently use a third-person point of view, using third-person pronouns (*he, she, they*)?
- Have I varied my sentence structure and the length of my sentences? Apply these specific questions where appropriate:

  > Where should I make some sentences longer by using conjunctions to connect independent clauses, dependent clauses, and phrases?

  > Where should I make some sentences shorter by separating any independent clauses?

- Did I follow the conventions of standard English including:

  > grammar?

  > spelling?

  > capitalization?

  > punctuation?

 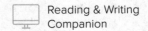

↻ YOUR TURN

Choose the best answer to each question.

1. The following is from a previous draft of Samrah's essay. How can the underlined sentence be rewritten in a more formal style?

> When Monk tries to grab Melvin, Priscilla puts him in a hammer lock. <u>If this doesn't make you laugh, I don't know what will.</u>

- ○ A. This is definitely the funniest part of the book.
- ○ B. Priscilla is brave.
- ○ C. You will laugh when reading this part.
- ○ D. Students will laugh out loud reading this story while witnessing bravery in action.

2. How can the following sentences be rewritten into more varied sentences, in keeping with a formal style?

> Priscilla is from "Priscilla and the Wimps." She is also young and brave. In the text it states she "hardly says anything to anybody." But she takes action and speaks up. She does this when her friend gets bullied.

- ○ A. Priscilla is. From "Priscilla and the Wimps." She is also young and brave. In the text it states she "hardly says anything to anybody," but she takes action and speaks up when her friend gets bullied.
- ○ B. Priscilla is from "Priscilla and the Wimps." She is also young and brave. But she takes action and speaks up when her friend gets bullied. Don't you think standing up to other kids is intimidating?
- ○ C. Priscilla, from "Priscilla and the Wimps," is also young and brave. In the text it states she "hardly says anything to anybody," but she takes action and speaks up when her friend gets bullied.
- ○ D. Priscilla, from "Priscilla and the Wimps," is also young and brave and in the text it states she "hardly says anything to anybody" but she takes action and speaks up when her friend gets bullied.

YOUR TURN

Complete the chart below by revising your draft to use a more formal and academic style. Look for areas in your draft in which you can vary the length of your sentences and use domain-specific language.

Style	Revised Sentence
Academic/formal style	
Varied sentence length and structure	
Domain-specific language	

Skill:
Conclusions

••• CHECKLIST FOR CONCLUSIONS

Before you write your conclusion, ask yourself the following questions:

- How can I restate the thesis or main idea in my concluding section or statement? What impression can I make on my reader?
- How can I write my conclusion so that it follows logically from my argument?
- Should I include a call to action?
- How can I conclude with a memorable comment?

Below are two strategies to help you provide a concluding statement or section that follows from the argument presented:

- Peer Discussion

  > after you have written your introduction and body paragraphs, talk with a partner and tell them what you want readers to remember, writing notes about your discussion

  > review your notes and think about what you wish to express in your conclusion

  > do not simply restate your claim or thesis statement. Rephrase your main idea to show the depth of your knowledge, the importance of your idea, and encourage readers to adopt your view.

  > write your conclusion

- Freewriting

  > freewrite for 10 minutes about what you might include in your conclusion. Don't worry about grammar, punctuation, or having fully formed ideas. The point of freewriting is to discover ideas.

  > review your notes and think about what you wish to express in your conclusion

  > do not simply restate your claim or thesis statement. Rephrase your main idea to show the depth of your knowledge, the importance of your idea, and encourage readers to adopt your view.

  > write your conclusion

YOUR TURN

Choose the best answer to each question.

1. The following conclusion is from an earlier draft of Samrah's essay. How can she rewrite the first, underlined sentence to better restate her thesis?

> <u>Both of these texts should be read by the book club.</u> Malala faced threats and was nearly killed for wanting to go to school. She survived and now speaks to the world. In the text it states that when she speaks, it's in "the voice of those 66 million girls" that can't go to school. She is determined and brave. Priscilla is different. She's a loner who "was sort of above everything," but when her one friend is threatened, she takes on the school bully. Her act of bravery helps out the other kids. We should read these texts in our book club because they show how you have to be brave to stand up for what's right. If you want to get an education, you might have to fight for it. If you want freedom from bullies, sometimes you have to get tough. These are lessons in bravery that we can all benefit from.

- ○ A. These texts are the best for learning about bravery.
- ○ B. These texts teach about bravery, and therefore are the best choice for our book club.
- ○ C. If you want to learn about bravery, you should totally pick these books for the book club.
- ○ D. Have you ever wanted to learn how to be brave?

2. Which sentence includes a call to action?

> (1) Her act of bravery helps out the other kids. (2) We should read these texts in our book club because they show how you have to be brave to stand up for what's right. (3) If you want to get an education, you might have to fight for it. (4) These are lessons in bravery that we can all benefit from.

- ○ A. sentence 1
- ○ B. sentence 2
- ○ C. sentence 3
- ○ D. sentence 4

 WRITE

Use the questions in the checklist to revise the conclusion of your literary analysis.

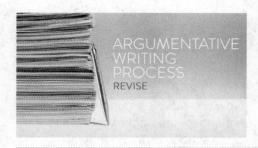

Argumentative Writing Process: Revise

PLAN	DRAFT	REVISE	EDIT AND PUBLISH

You have written a draft of your proposal. You have also received input from your peers about how to improve it. Now you are going to revise your draft.

◀◀ REVISION GUIDE

Examine your draft to find areas for revision. Keep in mind your purpose and audience as you revise for clarity, development, organization, and style. Use the guide below to help you review:

Review	Revise	Example
Clarity		
Highlight any place in your proposal where irrelevant information or sentence structure hinders clarity.	Revise sentences to remove irrelevant information and make the meaning clear.	"Priscilla and the Wimps" is an entertaining short story, ~~written by Richard Peck,~~ about a girl, named Priscilla, who stands up to a gang called "Klutter's Kobras." ~~The Kobras are led by Monk Klutter, who terrifies the kids at school by collecting money from them. They're afraid of Monk and his gang. They~~ The gang, led by Monk Klutter, forces kids to pay up so they don't get "barred from the school cafeteria" or worse.

Please note that excerpts and passages in the StudySync® library and this workbook are intended as touchstones to generate interest in an author's work. The excerpts and passages do not substitute for the reading of entire texts, and StudySync® strongly recommends that students seek out and purchase the whole literary or informational work in order to experience it as the author intended. Links to online resellers are available in our digital library. In addition, complete works may be ordered through an authorized reseller by filling out and returning to StudySync® the order form enclosed in this workbook.

Reading & Writing Companion   121

Review	Revise	Example
Development		
Identify places where you need to provide additional reasons or relevant evidence to support your thesis or main idea.	Focus on a single idea and add reasons, descriptions, details, evidence, or examples to support your idea.	Now she travels around the world fighting for the right of children to go to school. ~~in her country of Pakistan and all around the world.~~ She tells the stories of children who live in Nigeria, India, and Syria. These are places where war or certain beliefs keep kids, especially girls, from going to school.
Organization		
Review whether your text structure supports your purpose. Annotate places where the organization can be improved.	Rewrite information within paragraphs to improve organization.	~~Priscilla is quiet, large, and strong.~~ When one of the Kobras attacks Priscilla's only friend, Melvin, she steps in. Priscilla is quiet, large, and strong. With one "chop," she "breaks the Kobra's hold on Melvin's throat."
Style: Word Choice		
Identify places where stronger words or phrases would make your arguments more persuasive.	Select sentences to rewrite using words or phrases that appeal to emotions or logic.	Any kid who's ever been bullied or just felt ~~left out~~ like an underdog will find this story interesting and satisfying to read.
Style: Sentence Variety		
Review your proposal for choppiness. Create a better flow by combining some short sentences with transitions.	Rewrite choppy sentences to form more complex ones, using transitions when applicable.	She calls the Kobra a ~~"wimp." She~~ "wimp" and says she doesn't even know who Monk Klutter is.

✏ **WRITE**

Use the guide above, as well as your peer reviews, to help you evaluate your proposal to determine areas that should be revised.

Argumentative Writing Process: Edit and Publish

PLAN	DRAFT	REVISE	EDIT AND PUBLISH

You have revised your proposal based on your peer feedback and your own examination.

Now, it is time to edit your proposal. When you revised, you focused on the content of your proposal. You probably looked at your proposal's thesis statement, introduction and conclusion, organizational structure, style, transitions, reasons, and relevant evidence. When you edit, you focus on the mechanics of your proposal, paying close attention to things like grammar and punctuation.

Use the checklist below to guide you as you edit:

☐ Have I used commas correctly with nonessential elements?

☐ Have I used pronouns correctly?

☐ Have I been careful not to confuse *its* and *it's*, as well as *affect* and *effect*?

☐ Do I have any sentence fragments or run-on sentences?

☐ Have I spelled everything correctly?

Notice some edits Samrah has made:

- Added commas to set off nonessential elements.

- Replaced incorrect pronouns.

- Replaced *effect* with *affect* and *its* with *it's*.

Please note that excerpts and passages in the StudySync® library and this workbook are intended as touchstones to generate interest in an author's work. The excerpts and passages do not substitute for the reading of entire texts, and StudySync® strongly recommends that students seek out and purchase the whole literary or informational work in order to experience it as the author intended. Links to online resellers are available in our digital library. In addition, complete works may be ordered through an authorized reseller by filling out and returning to StudySync® the order form enclosed in this workbook.

Reading & Writing Companion   123

Both of these texts tell a story that will ~~effect~~ affect readers. However, what is most important is how each text teaches a message: You don't have to be an adult or big and powerful to be brave. We kids complain a lot about school; however, Malala's speech might make ~~them~~ us see things differently. Malala recovered. She won the Nobel Peace Prize. Now she travels around the world fighting for the right of children to go to school. She tells the stories of children who live in Nigeria, India, and Syria. These are places where war or certain beliefs keep kids, especially girls, from going to school. Her speech is worth reading because ~~its~~ it's a reminder that an education is a right not every kid in the world enjoys. ~~It's~~ Its message might make us feel more grateful for our school.

Priscilla, from "Priscilla and the Wimps," is also young and brave. In the text it states she "hardly says anything to anybody," but ~~he~~ she takes action and speaks up when her friend gets bullied. Sometimes standing up to other kids can be intimidating. The narrator of the story, one of the scared kids, calls Priscilla's actions "a move of pure poetry." Priscilla inspires the narrator because she isn't afraid to take on the bad guys. Priscilla will certainly have that ~~affect~~ effect on readers, too. Any kid who's ever been bullied or just felt like an underdog will find this story interesting and satisfying to read.

✎ WRITE

Use the questions above, as well as your peer reviews, to help you evaluate your proposal to determine areas that need editing. Then edit your proposal to correct those errors.

Once you have made all your corrections, you are ready to publish your work. You can distribute your writing to family and friends, hang it on a bulletin board, or post it on your blog. If you publish online, share the link with your family, friends, and classmates.

A Story of the South

Introduction

Imagine moving to another state and suddenly being ordered to leave a train station or sit at the back of a bus simply because of the color of your skin. How would you feel? How would you respond? These are the experiences and challenges faced by thirteen-year-old James Roberson, an African American boy growing up in the 1950's, whose family is forced to move from Ohio to Alabama at

VOCABULARY

treatment

the way that someone acts toward another person

surrender

to give up control or possession of

whim

a sudden desire

rebellion

uprisings against a government

elderly

older

terrifying

extremely frightening

 NOTES

READ

1   James Roberson's mother wanted to leave the South. She could not bear the racial hostility of the 1950s. The family moved to Ohio. There, James was judged by his southern accent rather than the color of his skin. The kids nicknamed him "Alabama," and they respected him because he was a good student. Then James and his family had to return to the South. James' dad could not find a job.

2   The train stopped in Decatur, Alabama, on the way back. James got off the train. He went into the station to get a snack. A woman suddenly shouted, "Get out of here!" James was stunned by this **treatment**. The woman had judged him on the color of his skin. He dashed back to the train and told his mother what had happened. She explained that black people in the South were not allowed in "all white" areas like the train station.

3   James quickly learned about discrimination. City buses in Birmingham, Alabama, were segregated based on city laws and the **whim** of the bus driver. Each bus had a green, wooden board. It fit on the back of bus seats. The board said, "Colored, do not sit beyond this board." The driver could decide any time to move the board. He could move it closer to the back of the bus. Then blacks sitting in front had to give up their seats to white people. An **elderly** black person might have to **surrender** his seat to a healthy white child.

4   When James was a teenager, he and his friends would throw the board away. They did this in **rebellion** against segregation. Sometimes they would sit right behind the bus driver. The driver would tell them to move. When they wouldn't, he would get off the bus and call for help. James and his friends would sneak off and disappear.

5   James was a member of a church led by Reverend Shuttlesworth. In 1956, the church parsonage was bombed. James lived nearby. The **terrifying** explosion broke windows in his house. The reverend surprisingly escaped injury. Armed blacks quickly gathered. James listened as the reverend urged people not to be violent.

A STORY OF THE SOUTH

First Read

Read the story. After you read, answer the Think Questions below.

☁ THINK QUESTIONS

1. Who is the main character in the story?

   The main character in the story is _____.

2. Write two or three sentences describing the setting of the story.

   The setting of the story_____

   _____.

3. At the end of the story, why were people worried?

   People were worried because _____

   _____.

4. Use context to confirm the meaning of the word *rebellion* as it is used in "A Story of the South." Write your definition of *rebellion* here.

   Rebellion means _____

   A context clue is _____

5. What is another way to say that a person is *elderly*?

   A person is _____.

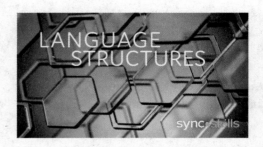

Skill:
Language Structures

⭐ **DEFINE**

In every language, there are rules that tell how to **structure** sentences. These rules define the correct order of words. In the English language, for example, a **basic** structure for sentences is subject, verb, and object. Some sentences have more **complicated** structures.

You will encounter both basic and complicated **language structures** in the classroom materials you read. Being familiar with language structures will help you better understand the text.

••• **CHECKLIST FOR LANGUAGE STRUCTURES**

To improve your comprehension of language structures, do the following:

✓ Monitor your understanding.

- Ask yourself: Why do I not understand this sentence? Is it because I do not understand some of the words? Or is it because I do not understand the way the words are ordered in the sentence?

✓ Pay attention to **perfect tenses** as you read. There are three perfect tenses in the English language: the present perfect, past perfect, and future perfect.

- **Present perfect tense** can be used to indicate a situation that began at a prior point in time and continues into the present.

  > Combine *have* or *has* with the past participle of the main verb.
  > Example: **I have played** basketball for three years.

- **Past perfect tense** can describe an action that happened before another action or event in the past.

  > Combine *had* with the past participle of the main verb.
  > Example: **I had learned** how to dribble a ball before I could walk!

> **Future perfect tense** expresses one future action that will begin and end before another future event begins or before a certain time.

> Use *will have* or *shall have* with the past participle of a verb.
> Example: Before the end of the year, **I will have played** more than 100 games!
> Example: By the time you play your first game, **I will have played** 100 games!

✓ Break down the sentence into its parts.

- Ask yourself: What actions are expressed in this sentence? Are they completed or are they ongoing? What words give me clues about when an action is taking place?

✓ Confirm your understanding with a peer or teacher.

⟳ YOUR TURN

Read each sentence in the first column. Write the action that happened first into the middle column. Write the action that happened second into the last column.

Sentences	First Past Action	Second Past Action
The class had stopped talking when the teacher walked into the room.		
When you arrived at the table, I had already finished my lunch.		
Jack likes Brazil's soccer team, so I gave him the jersey that I had bought in Brazil last month.		
My sister and I had cleaned our rooms before our mother asked us.		

Skill: Developing Background Knowledge

★ DEFINE

Developing background knowledge is the process of gaining information about different topics. By developing your background knowledge, you will be able to better understand a wider variety of texts.

First, preview the text to determine what the text is about. To **preview** the text, read the title, headers, and other text features and look at any images or graphics. As you are previewing, identify anything that is unfamiliar to you and that seems important.

While you are reading, you can look for clues that will help you learn more about any unfamiliar words, phrases, or topics. You can also look up information in another resource to increase your background knowledge.

••• CHECKLIST FOR DEVELOPING BACKGROUND KNOWLEDGE

To develop your background knowledge, do the following:

✓ Preview the text. Read the title, headers, and other features. Look at any images and graphics.

✓ Identify any words, phrases, or topics that you do not know a lot about.

✓ As you are reading, try to find clues in the text that give you information about any unfamiliar words, phrases, or topics.

✓ If necessary, look up information in other sources to learn more about any unfamiliar words, phrases, or topics. You can also ask a peer or teacher for information or support.

✓ Think about how the background knowledge you have gained helps you better understand the text.

⟳ YOUR TURN

Read each quotation from "A Story of the South." Imagine how you could develop your background knowledge. Write the letter of each strategy into the correct row.

	Strategy
A	You read an article about the Montgomery Bus Boycott.
B	You look at a map of the United States and find 'Ohio' and 'Alabama.'
C	You learn that your grandmother used trains to travel in 1950s.

Quotation	Strategy
"The family moved to Ohio. There, James was judged by his southern accent rather than the color of his skin. The kids nicknamed him 'Alabama,' and they respected him because he was a good student."	
"The train stopped in Decatur, Alabama, on the way back. James got off the train. He went into the station to get a snack."	
"City buses in Birmingham, Alabama, were segregated based on city laws and the whim of the bus driver."	

Close Read

 WRITE

INFORMATIONAL: In this text, James and his friends participated in several forms of "nonviolent protests" when riding the bus. Write a paragraph explaining what it means to participate in a nonviolent protest. Use details and examples from the text and your own background knowledge to support your ideas. Pay attention to spelling patterns and rules as you write.

Use the checklist below to guide you as you write.

☐ What is an injustice you experienced?

☐ How did you feel while it was happening?

☐ How did you react? What did you do?

Use the sentence frames to organize and write your informational paragraph.

An unjust experience that I had is _____.

It happened when _____.

I felt very _____.

I thought _____.

I reacted by _____.

It helped me _____.

Who's the Real Hero?

ARGUMENTATIVE
TEXT

Introduction

Two writers try to answer the question: What is a hero? The first writer believes that a hero must be special. Many of the people we call heroes are merely human, but a real hero must have more. After all, heroes from history fought and died for others. The second writer believes that heroes may simply be good people who do good things. That writer does not believe that heroes belong to an exclusive club. Instead, we may find heroes right in our own backyards!

VOCABULARY

designated

called by a particular name or title

venerate

to treat with great respect and admiration

merely

only; and nothing more

exclusive

open only to a select group

charitable

merciful or kind

NOTES

☰ READ

1 **Pro: Heroes Should Be Extraordinary**

2 It is boring to read yet another story about a local hero. The track star who runs like the wind is a hero. The woman who saved her own dog from a pond is a hero. Even a dog can be **designated** a hero, come to think of it. People love stories about brave dogs. The smoke alarm beeps. The dog barks. That doesn't seem heroic. It's more about saving oneself!

3 We should pick our heroes more carefully. Once, heroes were kings. They fought and died for others. Heroes' actions should be bold and brilliant. Did you invent a cure for cancer? You could be a hero. Did you yell, "Watch out for the car?" Not so much.

4 If an action is **merely** human, let's not call it heroic. If you see a falling brick, it's human to warn someone. If your dog falls in the water, it is **charitable** to help it out. These are acts that are part of being human. We should all be capable of such acts.

NOTES

5 Rosa Parks was a hero. She risked her freedom to help others gain theirs. Stephen Hawking is a hero. He does amazing science from a wheelchair. Salvatore Guinta is a hero. He risked his life to save the members of his army squad. He won the Medal of Honor for his actions. Can you live up to their examples? You could be a hero. Did you make a basket that won the game? Not so much.

6 **Con: A Hero May Be Quite Ordinary**

7 For good reason, we **venerate** the work of soldiers. We admire firefighters. We appreciate our Founders. However, they aren't the only heroes we have. We should not set the bar too high. We might miss the heroes right in our own backyard.

8 Imagine a single mom. Her dreams are on hold, but her children are well fed and educated. She is a hero. Imagine a student athlete. He does well in school and on the ball field. He is a hero. Heroism is about honor, sacrifice, and excellence. It shouldn't be an **exclusive** club. Many people have what it takes to be heroes.

9 A true hero should be a mirror that we hold up to ourselves. A true hero should make us want to be better than we are. The ordinary hero gives us something to live up to. We want to be like him or her, and we can.

First Read

Read the story. After you read, answer the Think Questions below.

Copyright © BookheadEd Learning, LLC

☁ THINK QUESTIONS

1. Whom does the first writer name as true heroes?

   The writer names _____

   _____.

2. Write two or three sentences describing why a single mom and a student athlete can be heroes.

   A single mom and a student athlete can be heroes because _____

   _____.

3. According to the second writer, what should a true hero do?

   A true hero should _____

   _____.

4. Use context to confirm the meaning of the word *exclusive* as it is used in "Who's the Real Hero?" Write your definition of *exclusive* here.

   Exclusive means _____.

   A context clue is _____.

5. What is another way to say that a person is *charitable*?

   A person is _____.

Skill:
Analyzing Expressions

★ DEFINE

When you read, you may find English expressions that you do not know. An **expression** is a group of words that communicates an idea. Three types of expressions are idioms, sayings and figurative language They can be difficult to understand because the meanings of the words are different from their **literal**, or usual, meanings.

An **idiom** is an expression that is commonly known among a group of people. For example: "It's raining cats and dogs" means it is raining heavily. **Sayings** are short expressions that contain advice or wisdom. For instance, "Don't count your chickens before they hatch" means do not plan on something good happening before it happens. **Figurative** language is when you describe something by comparing it with something else, either directly (using the words *like* or *as*) or indirectly. For example, "I'm hungry as a horse" means I'm very hungry. None of these expressions are about actual animals.

••• CHECKLIST FOR ANALYZING EXPRESSIONS

To determine the meaning of an expression, remember the following:

✓ If you find a confusing group of words, it may be an expression. The meaning of words in expressions may not be their literal meaning.

- Ask yourself: Is this confusing because the words are new? Or because the words do not make sense together?

✓ Determining the overall meaning may require that you use one or more of the following:

- context clues

- a dictionary or other resource

- teacher or peer support

✓ Highlight important information before and after the expression to look for clues.

Please note that excerpts and passages in the StudySync® library and this workbook are intended as touchstones to generate interest in an author's work. The excerpts and passages do not substitute for the reading of entire texts, and StudySync® strongly recommends that students seek out and purchase the whole literary or informational work in order to experience it as the author intended. Links to online resellers are available in our digital library. In addition, complete works may be ordered through an authorized reseller by filling out and returning to StudySync® the order form enclosed in this workbook.

Reading & Writing Companion   **139**

YOUR TURN

Read the following excerpt from the text. Then, complete the multiple-choice questions below.

---

from **"Who's the Real Hero?"**

It is boring to read yet another story about a local hero. The track star who <u>runs like the wind</u> is a hero. The woman who saved her own dog from a pond is a hero. Even a dog can be designated a hero, come to think of it. People love stories about brave dogs. The smoke alarm beeps. The dog barks. That doesn't seem heroic. It's more about saving oneself!

---

1. What does it mean to "run like the wind"?

    ○ A. make noise as you run
    ○ B. run where the wind blows
    ○ C. run extremely quickly
    ○ D. use your arms to help you run

2. A context clue that helps you understand the expression "runs like the wind" is:

    ○ A. another story
    ○ B. local hero
    ○ C. track star
    ○ D. saved her own dog

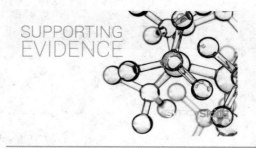

Skill:
Supporting Evidence

★ DEFINE

In some informational or argumentative texts, the author may share an opinion. This **opinion** may be the author's **claim** or **thesis**. The author must then provide readers with **evidence** that supports their opinion. Supporting evidence can be details, examples, or facts that agree with the author's claim or thesis.

Looking for supporting evidence can help you confirm your understanding of what you read. Finding and analyzing supporting evidence can also help you form your own opinions about the subject.

••• CHECKLIST FOR SUPPORTING EVIDENCE

In order to find and analyze supporting evidence, do the following:

✓ Identify the topic and the author's claim or thesis.

- Ask yourself: What is this mostly about? What is the author's opinion?

✓ Find details, facts, and examples that support the author's claim or thesis.

- Ask yourself: Is this detail important? How does this detail relate to the thesis or claim?

✓ Analyze the supporting evidence.

- Ask yourself: Is this evidence strong? Do I agree with the evidence?

Please note that excerpts and passages in the StudySync® library and this workbook are intended as touchstones to generate interest in an author's work. The excerpts and passages do not substitute for the reading of entire texts, and StudySync® strongly recommends that students seek out and purchase the whole literary or informational work in order to experience it as the author intended. Links to online resellers are available in our digital library. In addition, complete works may be ordered through an authorized reseller by filling out and returning to StudySync® the order form enclosed in this workbook.

Reading & Writing Companion   **141**

YOUR TURN

Read the following excerpt from the text. Then, complete the multiple choice questions below.

---

from "Who's the Real Hero?"

Imagine a single mom. Her dreams are on hold, but her children are well fed and educated. She is a hero. Imagine a student athlete. He does well in school and on the ball field. He is a hero. Heroism is about honor, sacrifice, and excellence. It shouldn't be an exclusive club. Many people have what it takes to be heroes.

---

1. What is the author's claim?

   ○ A. Heroes are athletic and strong.
   ○ B. Heroes can be ordinary people.
   ○ C. Heroes are in an exclusive club.
   ○ D. Heroes should be well educated.

2. What examples does the author give as evidence?

   ○ A. Children who are well fed
   ○ B. A single mom and a student athlete
   ○ C. Many people who have what it takes
   ○ D. Anyone who has sacrificed for others

3. What actions are provided as evidence of "sacrifice"?

   ○ A. Putting dreams on hold for one's children
   ○ B. Feeding children while she goes hungry
   ○ C. Succeeding on the baseball field
   ○ D. Doing well in school and getting an education

4. What actions are provided as evidence of "excellence"?

   ○ A. Making sure that children are well fed
   ○ B. Attending the best possible schools
   ○ C. Surviving as a single mother
   ○ D. Being successful in academics and athletics

WHO'S THE REAL HERO?

Close Read

Copyright © BookheadEd Learning, LLC

✏️ WRITE

ARGUMENTATIVE: What do you think it takes to be a hero? Write a paragraph explaining your opinion. Use evidence from the text and from your own personal experience to support your argument. Pay attention to using negatives and contractions correctly as you write.

Use the checklist below to guide you as you write.

☐ Who are some of your personal heroes?

☐ Which text argument do your personal heroes more closely match?

☐ How would you describe heroism?

Use the sentence frames to organize and write your argument.

To be a hero, you should _____

_____.

For example, heroes should be _____

_____.

In my experience, real heroes _____

_____.

An example of a true hero, in my opinion, might be _____

_____

_____, because _____

_____

PHOTO/IMAGE CREDITS:

studysync®

Text Fulfillment Through StudySync

If you are interested in specific titles, please fill out the form below and we will check availability through our partners.

ORDER DETAILS

Date:

TITLE	AUTHOR	Paperback/ Hardcover	Specific Edition *If Applicable*	Quantity

SHIPPING INFORMATION

Contact:

Title:

School/District:

Address Line 1:

Address Line 2:

Zip or Postal Code:

Phone:

Mobile:

Email:

BILLING INFORMATION   ☐ *SAME AS SHIPPING*

Contact:

Title:

School/District:

Address Line 1:

Address Line 2:

Zip or Postal Code:

Phone:

Mobile:

Email:

PAYMENT INFORMATION

☐ CREDIT CARD

Name on Card:

Card Number: Expiration Date: Security Code:

☐ PO

Purchase Order Number:

StudySync Text Fulfillment, BookheadEd Learning, LLC
610 Daniel Young Drive I Sonoma, CA 95476